# YOU ARE MY
# LARSSON

## Mark Guidi and
## Ewing Grahame

# YOU ARE MY LARSSON

Published by the Daily Record and Sunday Mail,
One Central Quay, Glasgow, G3 8DA.
Copyright: The Daily Record

ISBN
0-9513471-1-X

Printed and bound in Scotland

MARK GUIDI is Chief Football Writer of the Sunday Mail. He has worked with Scotland's biggest selling newspaper since 1995.

He also works as a football analyst for Radio Clyde's Super Scoreboard programme.

Mark was previously with Scottish Football Today magazine, 7-Day-Press, Today and Radio Scotland.

He lives with wife Anne and daughter Eva.

EWING GRAHAME has been a sports reporter since 1977, writing for the Weekly News, Sunday Post, Sunday Scot, Scotland On Sunday, the Sunday Times, the Observer, the Sun, the Daily Record and the Herald.

He is married to Aileen and has three children (Rachel, Niamh and Dylan). In his limited spare time Ewing is a historian, specialising in the life and times of Elvis Aaron Presley (1935-77) and Francis Albert Sinatra(1915-98). Probably.

# CONTENTS

# introduction

HENRIK LARSSON was anything but a household name when
Wim Jansen brought him to Celtic Park on July 25, 1997, for just
£650,000 from Dutch club Feyenoord.

But it became apparent very quickly that the Swedish striker had
enormous talent and would turn out to be a bargain buy.

He helped Celtic win the Coca-Cola Cup that season and, more
importantly, the League Championship to stop a Rangers side that
had dominated Scottish football for almost a decade.

Since then, Larsson has lifted another League Cup and his 53
goals last season helped Celtic to their first Treble since 1969 and
won him the prestigious UEFA Golden Shoe award for Europe's
most prolific goalscorer.

The way Henrik conducts himself on and off the park has made
him a favourite of the Celtic support – along with fans up and down
the country – and he is rated by many as one of the most consistent
strikers to ever wear the green and white hoops.

But it hasn't been all smiles during the star striker's four years in
Glasgow with wife Magdalena and son Jordan. He broke a leg
against Lyon in a UEFA Cup tie on October 21, 1999, and was
ruled out for the next six months.

But brave Henrik fought back to full fitness to have his greatest
season last year under Martin O'Neill and celebrated with the
signing of a lucrative new contract, tying him to the club until 2004.

The book you are about to read is a well-deserved tribute to this
fine man and gives an unprecedented insight into a superstar,
on and off the park. Footballing people such as Jansen, Kenny
Dalglish, Paolo di Canio, Brian Laudrup, Craig Brown, Murdo
MacLeod and Marc Rieper have their say as well as ordinary
men and women who have shared his company. Read and enjoy...

# one the early years

HENRIK Larsson was born on the 20th of September, 1971, in Helsingborg, a small, football-mad Swedish city.

His father, Francisco Rocha, was a sailor from the Cape Verde islands, a batch of territories just off the West Coast of Africa that were once under Portuguese rule.

Rocha met and fell in love with Eva Larsson, a factory worker, when his ship put ashore in Sweden.

They quickly set up home together and Francisco also started to work in a factory. They have two children, Henrik and his younger brother Robert. Eva already had a son Kim, whose father was Lebanese. But in their hearts Henrik and Robert regard all three as full brothers.

His parents decided to give Henrik his mother's surname as they thought it would help to have as much of a Swedish identity as possible.

But it wasn't enough to prevent the boy suffering racial abuse at school because his skin wasn't white.

Henrik was always small for his age and weighed much less than most of his classmates. However, from an early age he displayed the kind of aggression and strength he now has as a top footballer. As a kid, he used to bloody a few noses when fellow pupils taunted him by calling him 'nigger'. But young Larsson's reputation increased as he proved himself in different sports and his tormentors eventually left him alone, not wanting to come into contact with his fists again.

As his love for football grew, Pele became Henrik's hero. Part of the reason he worshipped the Brazilian was because he was black and the youngster used to engross himself night after night watching the great man's video.

The racist chants have continued to follow Larsson during his career. England fans verbally abused him at the Euro 2000 qualifier in Stockholm – which Sweden won 2-1 – leading to the English FA being fined.

He has since taken part in anti-racism videos to show how much he detests it.

But Henke, as he is affectionately known in his homeland, can have no complaints about his career and would be the first to admit he has been blessed with good fortune.

His father presented him with his first ball when he was just 16 months old; he was dribbling with it days later. Henrik hasn't looked back from that moment.

He was very close to his father and used to beg Francisco to take him to see organised matches. Dad eventually gave in and took Henrik to see Helsingborgs watch Watford when he was five years old. But the visit turned into a nightmare as the youngster continually fidgeted, to the annoyance of the other spectators, and his father had to take him home before the game had finished. Henke was simply bored and rather than sit watching wanted to be out there kicking the ball.

Larsson used to practise night and day outside his humble high-rise block of flats in Narlunda, on the outskirts of Helsingborg, with his best friend Fredrik Bjork.

Bjork, now a schoolteacher, recalled Henke's talent and dedication: "We grew up in the same building and our families were good friends.

"We played football from as far back as I can remember. Our first real club was Hogaborg when we were six.

"But no matter what Henke might tell you, when we were

young I was the better player. He never really talked much about becoming a footballer but I had an idea he had it in his mind and was always determined to get what he wanted.

"However, I never imagined he would become a professional. Henke was just my friend. I don't know why we became pals, I suppose I knew I could trust him and count on him.

"Then, at about 16, he became very good and people started to think he could turn pro. He had other interests, too, such as ski-ing in the hills or hanging about down the youth centre.

"But football was always his first sport. I remember during the 1978 World Cup Final between Holland and Argentina, which went to extra-time, Henke called me and said he wanted to go out and play football right after the match. The drama of the game had got him all fired up.

"The first time I thought he really had a chance to go right to the top of the football tree was when he was 16 and scored all five goals in a 5-1 win."

Of course, Larsson has made it and is now rated one of the most lethal strikers in the United Kingdom. But he's come through some serious setbacks and the odds were stacked against him when he first started taking the game seriously.

He gave a glimpse of what was to lie ahead when he was just six and scored his first-ever goal in a proper game. It was for Hogaborg and, in true Henrik style, he flung himself through a crowd of players to head home bravely.

Larsson doesn't recall what his celebration was like but knows for sure it wasn't the tongue-out routine – his strict parents would have disciplined him for that. At 12, he was smaller than most of the players and often had to do with a place on the bench.

Some of his coaches only involved him in matches as a sympathy vote. But one, Bengt Persson, who sadly died last year, encouraged the boy and told the hopeful striker he would grow and had the talent to make a living from the game.

Henke took on board what his mentor said and made himself believe in those words.

Larsson recalled: "I have always adored football and used to love watching the English games on television on Saturday afternoons, especially when Liverpool and Spurs were involved. I liked Kenny Dalglish, Terry McDermott, Kevin Keegan and Ossie Ardiles. I just wanted to be like them.

"Some people thought I didn't have a chance and I had a bit of a hard time at school when I was younger. But I think being good at sport helped me.

"However, you have to work to make it to the top and I don't think at that age you realise the hard graft involved. There are so many talented players out there but you have to be dedicated as well as lucky. Being in the right place at the right time is also important.

"For years I thought I had a chance of becoming a professional but at 12 years old I seemed to stop growing. I was still very quick but the other boys found it easy to knock me off the ball. Bengt Persson took me aside one day and told me I had talent and not to worry. But he also told me talent is sometimes not always enough, you have to work hard as well. It's advice I've taken with me everywhere."

Larsson didn't always listen, though, and his teachers found it difficult to get through when it came to his studies. If it involved a kickabout or homework, there was only one winner.

And when the teachers used to ask the normal questions to their pupils such as 'What do you want to be when you grow up?' most would answer a fireman or a train driver, but young Henke always answered 'footballer'. His tutors thought he was on another planet.

Still, his old teachers don't mind their first impressions of young Henke being wrong. One of his first teachers at Wieselgrensskolan in Helsingborg, Lise-Lotte Johansson, remembers him well. She told him to stop being a dreamer, give up football and concentrate on schoolwork.

But Lisa knew she was hitting her head off a brick wall with single-minded Henke. She recalled: "He was only about eight or nine when I taught him maths and Swedish. I just wanted him to be realistic, not many boys make it as footballers.

"I told him not to count on football as he wouldn't make much money. Of course, I hadn't seen him play and I'm just glad he ignored my advice. I'm pleased he has lived out his dream.

"I will always remember him as a gorgeous young boy with

curly brown hair. But strangely, at the front one of his curls was white-blonde. If it weren't for that you might not have noticed him. He was so quiet and polite. I think all he wanted to do was blend in with the other boys."

German teacher Jan Gustavsson said: "Henke was quiet and unassuming but popular. German didn't hold much interest for him and we were used to hearing kids express impossible ambitions all the time. But I did go to see him play for Hogaborg and was taken aback by his talent on the pitch. None of us could have known he would make it as big as he did, but I had an idea he wouldn't give up wanting to be a footballer.

"After leaving school, and before his career took off, Henrik used to work in the school's recreation centre and we would have lunch together. Even then he was becoming a star but no-one really noticed because he was such a nice down-to-earth guy."

A lot of players who are stars are selfish, unhelpful and aloof. Larsson doesn't fall into any of those three categories and the people who have known him since his early days only have fond memories and pleasant stories to tell.

Leif Plume, one of the workers in the recreation centre, has nothing but admiration for Henrik. He said: "I used to play a game called floorball with Henke and he was brilliant. In fact, there were not many sports he didn't excel at.

"But he has always kept his nice manners and good upbringing, never forgetting his roots. I remember a few years ago my son fell and broke his leg and both arms. When Henke got to hear about it he made a point of visiting us during one of his trips to Sweden.

"My little boy was overwhelmed, Larsson is one of his heroes. But that is just typical of Henke. Even now that he is so famous and successful he hasn't forgotten where it all started or his friends from the past."

Apart from making other people's lives better, Larsson loved attention for his sporting achievements and liked nothing better than getting noticed for his skills.

Ann Bjorkman taught him Swedish for three years and said: "He wasn't very interested in reading or writing. When he wrote essays for my class they would often be about his dream of becoming a footballer. One Sunday my son was playing football and I noticed from the other match results that Henke had scored two goals. I congratulated him the next morning in school. He quite literally glowed with pride. It was obvious he was pleased I had noticed.

"Apart from football his only other dream was to go to Cape Verde, the birthplace of his father. Once Henke had left school I taught his younger brother Robert. They looked so alike and people would often mistake him for his older brother.

"I am very proud to see Henke doing so well and I remember watching Sweden against Bulgaria in the 1994 World Cup finals. I was in a bar in France but when Henke scored I couldn't help but start bragging that I knew him. Suddenly, everyone in the place wanted to talk to me.

"Now if any of my pupils are interested in football I will tell them about Henke. But it works both ways and I know he has not forgotten about me.

"About 10 years after he left school, I saw him in a local bar during a night out with his friends. He recognised me immediately and joked to his friends: 'Oh no, here comes my Swedish teacher'."

Those who know Larsson best will also testify that behind the goals and the stick-out tongue is a man with a wicked sense of humour which sometimes can be quite naughty. He likes practical jokes and keeping people on their toes, hoping to catch them out when they least expect it.

Another of the recreation workers, Annika Pramborn, was nicknamed Televinken by Henrik after a puppet character in a Swedish children's television programme.

She laughed: "I have a long nose and so did Televinken. It was a good-natured nickname, though. I didn't find it offensive. Henke was always a caring, generous young man and we've known each other since we were about 15. But when we left school we didn't see each other for many years.

"Then I was running a 10 kilometre race in Helsingborg and saw him standing among the spectators. As soon as he spotted me he shouted out 'Televinken, good luck'. I was so pleased he had remembered me because by that time he was getting quite famous. Success hasn't changed him one bit."

As Larsson excelled on the football pitch he became more

popular and was never short of friends or those wanting to be seen with him. But he wasn't fooled and could tell within a few minutes of meeting people if they were genuine or hangers-on.

One guy who did earn Henke's respect was Walle Holmberg, a school friend and now a journalist on the Helsingborgs Dagblad.

Walle has followed Henke's career closely and the pair meet up as often as their busy schedules allow. But their relationship was almost over before it began when Larsson took exception to an article written about him by Holmberg.

The journalist remembers the whole episode well and said: "Henrik has qualifications as a groundsman and often jokes that at least he has something to fall back on if playing football doesn't work out. Somehow, now, I don't think his other day job will be necessary.

"When he was about 14 or 15, he made his debut for the Hogaborg first team and I wrote an article about it. Henrik had scored a goal but I wrote he hadn't contributed much else for the rest of the game. He told me later that report had really annoyed him and he vowed never to speak to me again.

"Thankfully, he did but he also got his revenge on a training weekend in Cyprus in 1992. I was sitting at a table eating dinner when suddenly these big strong arms grabbed me from behind and threw me into the swimming pool, fully clothed. It was Henrik who had got a hold of me. It was then he told me about the report and said: 'That's my revenge'.

"But we have been close for a long time and I followed him out to Rotterdam when he first signed for Feyenoord because his girlfriend Magdalena had not yet joined him there. In the garden of his new house was a small shed. Henrik used to say he daren't go in there in case it had mice. He was scared of them.

"But I have nothing but respect and admiration for him. He has grown up a lot since he married Magdalena and had his son Jordan. Before Jordan, he didn't really need to have any responsibilities, Magdalena would would take care of everything, paying the bills and running errands."

Before Larsson moved to Dutch giants Feyenoord he really had worked his socks off and grafted hard to make sure he had money in his pocket before football provided him with a steady income. Apart from the recreation centre he took on jobs such as packing fruit and vegetables in a warehouse.

Henrik met Magdalena in a restaurant when he was 19 and they were soon dating. But it wasn't football that brought them together. Magdalena wasn't interested in the beautiful game at that time. She is now, of course.

Upmarket sports were her thing and she was then, and still is, a keen horse-rider. They decided to meet in the middle as their relationship blossomed and Henrik took up horse-riding while Magdalena attended games to cheer him on.

The couple married in Sweden six years later on a midsummer's eve and held their wedding reception in the Royal Gardens of Sofiero, the Swedish Royal Family's summer residence.

No doubt about it, Magdalena helped Henrik settle down. When they met he was playing football for Hogaborg and enjoying it. But it wasn't everything to him.

When Larsson speaks honestly he admits to believing his dream of becoming a professional might never happen because he knew that when you reach your early 20s and you haven't broken through, doubts creep in.

Then Henrik heard Helsingborgs, his home-town club, were interested in him and had been watching his progress. He was at work one day when he received a phone call from the club to tell him they wanted to speak with him. A friend drove him there and he signed immediately for £300 a month without bonuses.

But Hogaborg have continued to follow Larsson's career with pride and haven't forgotten his contribution. In his honour they now have the Henke-boll, an annual prize for the 16-year-old who performs most consistently over the season. Henrik has been known to return to his first club to present the prize.

The move to Helsingborgs was a turning point for the brilliant youngster. He started training seriously, scored 34 goals in his first season and the team won promotion to the first division for the first time in 22 years. Larsson formed a prolific partnership with former Swedish international striker Mats Magnusson and 6000 people flocked to the Helsingborg harbour to greet the team after their promotion.

Magnusson, a former Benfica star, recalled: "The reception was terrific with people waiting with banners and amazing celebrations. I managed to get myself a special souvenir from that night – I cut off one of Henrik's dreadlocks.

"I think I still have it in the house somewhere – it is like a big cigar. I am so pleased to see Henrik doing well in Scotland, he deserves it."

The chance to play in Sweden's top league was something Larsson craved. He was desperate to see how well he would measure up against the country's leading players and managed to score 16 times in his first season in the big league.

His skill helped the average home gate swell by 500 and, as his popularity grew, so did the amount of his posters hanging on the bedroom walls of female supporters attracted to his rasta looks.

Those two years at Helsingborgs will be forever etched in the superstar's mind. But in September 1993, it was time to move up to another level and he joined Feyenoord in a £295,000 deal.

# two feyenoord

MICHEL DOESBURG has watched Henrik progress from gawky youngster to grown man, from a promising talent to a fully-fledged superstar.

It's a journey the 33-year-old has been privileged to share and he's tracked his most difficult opponent all the way.

Doesburg was a journeyman defender with Heerenveen when Larsson moved from Helsingborgs to Wim Jansen's Feyenoord in 1993 and he enjoyed – if that's the correct word – tussles with him there and also with his next club, AZ Alkmaar.

Michel is unique. He has been able to pinpoint the blossoming of Henrik's remarkable career over the last eight years in Holland and in Scotland since he moved here to Motherwell and, currently, Dunfermline.

Larsson was just 21 when he made his £295,000 move to Rotterdam and half of that fee went to his first club Hogaborg. Doesburg insists – although there were signs that a unique talent was waiting to be unleashed to back Jansen's judgment in signing him – Henrik was nowhere near as brilliant as he is now.

Michel said: "He was already a good player when he came to

Holland but nothing like the world-class star he is now. Even then, though, Larsson was difficult to play against, although it's hard to make too many comparisons because I wasn't so good either in those days."

However, Henrik's team-mate and best friend at Feyenoord, Dutch defender Orlando Trustfull, was impressed from day one.

The 31-year-old, now with Vitesse Arnhem, grinned: "I'll never forget his first training session with us – he scored three goals which were out of this world.

"We told him right away he should go to Amsterdam and play for Ajax, who were top dogs then. We joked he was too good for Feyenoord.

"We were friends but every single member of our squad liked Henrik and our supporters loved him.

"The Ajax players walk around like stars with their noses stuck up in the air but Feyenoord has always been a people's club and Henrik likes to be a normal person, so he fitted in perfectly.

"He would always work his socks off, which the crowd loved, and we enjoyed playing alongside him – he would never let you down."

Everything went smoothly at first in Holland, even though Feyenoord were unable to hold on to the championship they had won the previous season.

But still Henrik was part of the team that beat NEC Nijmegen 2-1 to win the Dutch Cup, with goals from Ruud Heus and John van Loen.

By then Jansen, the man Larsson regards as his mentor, had decided to leave the club. He had been general manager and wanted to return to coaching, so when Leo Beenhakker offered him the chance to take charge of the Saudi Arabian national side he jumped at it.

Henrik may not have realised it at the time – things would get better before they got worse, after all – but Wim's departure signalled the beginning of the end of his Feyenoord career.

The following season Henrik, along with Ed de Goey, Ronald Koeman and Giovanni van Bronckhorst, was part of the side that lost 4-1 to Rapid Vienna in the European Cup-Winners' Cup semi-final.

By way of consolation Larsson was still in place for the 2-1 win over Volendam which saw them retain the Dutch Cup, the goals this time coming from Gustav Taument and Nigerian Mike Obiku.

The following season another Cup-Winners' Cup run was halted at the quarter-final stage by Real Zaragoza. Sadly for Henrik, though, the appointment of former World Cup hero Arie Haan as coach was to provide the young striker with almost 18 months of unmitigated misery.

In the European Football Who's Who for 200/2001, published by football bible World Soccer, Haan is tellingly (and diplomatically) referred to thus: "Tactically above average but not a coach who is in favour of dialogue with his players." As Larsson would be the first to tell you, that is something of an understatement.

It would be fair to say player and boss didn't bond. In fact, if they had anything at all in common it's still to arise.

At first Henrik put up with the baffling positional changes thrust on him by Haan, who would play him wide right one week, wide left the next and as target man for the match after that.

He was also regularly deployed in midfield and, while able to perform capably enough in that role, it was a criminal misuse of talent.

That lack of consistency would have been dispiriting enough but it was made worse by the fact that, irrespective of how well Larsson was playing, Haan would regularly substitute him – usually with an inferior player.

Trustfull said: "Henrik had a difficult time towards the end. He wasn't being played up front and wasn't getting the four or five games in a row you need for sharpness.

"He was asked to play behind the forwards, which obviously made it much harder for him to score. The most difficult thing for any player is when he doesn't have the support and trust of the coach, and the last six months were tough for him.

"I had just left for Sheffield Wednesday, although I kept in touch with Henrik then as I still do now.

"He made the right choice in leaving Feyenoord because he wasn't feeling good about himself. The problem was that Haan is an ignorant man.

"He thought he had personally invented football and it wasn't possible to have a conversation with him about anything.

"There was only one opinion allowed – his – and his way was the only way to do anything. Sometimes great players know what teams should be doing but they're not capable of explaining it. Haan comes into that category.

"It's true to say he wasn't popular with the rest of the players."

Michel Doesburg watched from the outside with interest and no little puzzlement. He said: "One of the reasons Henrik didn't develop there as he has since leaving Feyenoord was that the coach clearly had no faith in him.

"That is an important relationship for any player. If you're lucky enough to have a manager who believes in you it can make a huge difference to your game.

"It's also comforting to know you'll play every week and in, if not your best position, at least the same position.

"Henrik always had a good relationship with the Feyenoord fans, though, because they love players who give 100 per cent for their team and Larsson never gave anything less. They realised his worth even if the people running the club didn't.

"I would imagine now, though, there are directors watching him do so well for Celtic and Sweden who must be wondering how they ever allowed him to slip through their hands."

On his official website, the accoutrement no self-respecting superstar can afford to be without, Henrik said: "I saw myself as a striker but they were playing me everywhere.

"The Dutch press were on my back. I think they accepted I was talented but I just wasn't scoring the goals.

"It didn't upset me – I just stopped reading the papers – but I believe you have to enjoy your football."

Certainly, Larsson's relative failure with Feyenoord – and it's a failure better than most players' successes – could not be laid at his door. As Doesburg pointed out, he did everything he could to make things work.

Michel said: "When I first came to Scotland I already spoke good English but the first thing I did was to make a list of all the phrases I would need to know during a match – like 'man on!' and 'keeper's ball' – and learn them off by heart.

"One story is a great example of how professional Larsson is.

When he joined Feyenoord, Henrik and his wife immediately learned Dutch, one of the most difficult languages to grasp.

"Some foreigners when they arrive at a club need to be forced to learn the language. They refuse to attend classes. Some just don't bother at all.

"I watched the Champions League qualifying tie between Ajax and Celtic in Amsterdam on Dutch TV and almost all the interviews with Ajax's imported players were conducted in English because they couldn't do it in Dutch.

"Interestingly, before that match the Dutch commentators were saying that everybody in Holland was very happy as Shota Arveladze had been allowed to play by the club's directors because he had been Ajax's top scorer with 18 goals the previous season.

"At that point, my wife asked me how many goals Henrik had scored for Celtic – when I told her 53 we both burst out laughing.

"Even now when we are playing against each other Henrik and I always have a chat before the match – in Dutch of course."

Doesburg learned early on that Larsson is much, much tougher than he looks. However, it wasn't until both men were plying their trade in Scotland that it became painfully obvious.

On April 17, 1999 – the day before Henrik picked up his PFA Footballer of the Year award at Glasgow's Thistle Hotel – both men clashed at Celtic Park. Literally.

Michel, then a Motherwell player, had been told to keep Larsson quiet. Not for the first time it was a case of the biter bitten.

He recalled: "Henrik has always been a hard opponent but after that match I remember our boss, Billy Davies, complaining in the newspapers about a challenge he made on me.

"I was given a man-marking job to do on him and ended up with his stud marks on my leg. But so what? I was disappointed I couldn't come out for the second half but I had been kicking him too.

"Football is a man's game and strikers shouldn't allow themselves to be bullied. They should stand up the way Henrik does."

Insult was added to injury when Celtic grabbed the only goal of the game in the second half. Through Larsson, naturally.

Doesburg admits that when it comes to near-impossible tasks, attempting to shut out Celtic's greatest post-war striker is up there with trying to nail jelly to the ceiling.

He said: "You need to be focused all the time, you can't allow him a second on the ball. The guys who feed him at Celtic are great and his partnership with Chris Sutton is frightening, but ultimately it all comes down to Henrik.

"On the one hand you feel absolutely brilliant if you come off the park at the end of 90 minutes having stopped him scoring. The downside is he often scores several times.

"The biggest progress he has made since leaving Feyenoord is in his goal-scoring. As far as I'm concerned he's now world class.

"I remember playing against him at East End Park and with 15 minutes left we were one goal up. We came off at the end and Henrik hadn't played particularly well.

"Afterwards in the dressing-room my team-mates and I agreed we had done well. But we ended up losing 2-1 and he got both goals...

"Nowadays you are lucky to get away with a match against Larsson when he scores only once.

"He's not the tallest player but climbs to great heights when the ball is in the air. He has pace, he can finish and he has strength.

"He's one of a kind and I believe he could play in any league in the world. People say defenders in Serie A are killers but I've no doubts Henrik could handle them without a problem."

Which is exactly the kind of Dutch backing Larsson could have done with as he struggled through his final, unhappy season at Feyenoord.

During that campaign, which saw Feyenoord fail to capture a trophy, Henrik was worried at work and found it difficult not to take his problems home to Magdalena. It was a period he would prefer to forget but, with the benefit of hindsight, Trustfull believes the tribulations then have proved to be the making of him.

He said: "It was all part of the learning process – and Henrik learned a lot from it. Now he knows how to cope with any difficult situation.

"It made him what he is now so I think it's all been for the good, although the Feyenoord fans didn't like it. He's a different player now from the one I played with back then; cleverer, more mature. Although Henrik has great pace he now knows when it's best to take his time.

"You're never going to have success in football if you aren't happy and that is why he is doing so well now. I've been to Celtic Park to watch him play and to say the fans there love him doesn't begin to tell the story."

Larsson's Dutch difficulties saw him hit a lull in his international fortunes but Swedish strike partner Kennet Andersson also believes it was enduring that hellish time in Rotterdam that finally set the hitman on the road to greatness.

Andersson claimed: "It's easy to say now but I think those last years Henrik spent in Holland were the most important of his entire career.

"I had a very similar experience when I was 24 and playing, or not playing, for the Belgian club Mechelen in 1991. When you come back from a bad experience like that you know not to take anything for granted in the future. That's the positive side of it.

"You know you have to work for your success and what Henrik went through with Feyenoord helps you to enjoy happiness when it comes.

"As a human being it's important every now and then to have some kind of problem to solve. It makes you a better person.

"Henrik has shown by the way he has bounced back from his disappointments that he is strong mentally. He really is an extraordinary man."

Back then, though, Larsson was made to feel very ordinary indeed by Haan (last heard of coaching Greek minnows Paniliakos, which may or may not be a source of satisfaction in Henrik's household).

As week followed depressing week, the realisation dawned that things would not improve unless one of the two men left. Larsson decided he would be the one to go.

Enter an unlikely hero, stage right. Henrik's relationship with the media is, it's fair to say, on the cool side.

He holds interviews only when he needs to and doesn't do the lunch thing with members of the Fourth Estate. Yet we can reveal in these pages for the first time that it was a journalist who was directly responsible for the move to Celtic.

Marcel van der Kram, a sports reporter based in Rotterdam, is the man every Hoops fan must thank for bringing their idol to Parkhead.

He said: "At the time Henrik was very unhappy. He didn't think he was getting any respect from coach Haan and was also given no support by the President, Jorien van den Herik.

"However, I knew he had a clause in his contract that allowed him to go abroad for a set fee. Coincidentally, Wim Jansen had just been appointed head coach of Celtic.

"That was the point when I gave Wim a call and told him that if he was looking for a quality striker, I knew of one who was available..."

# three the transfer

MARCEL VAN DER KRAM'S phone call to Wim Jansen
proved to be merely the first step on what was to become a long,
anxious journey before the 500 miles between Rotterdam and
Glasgow were safely negotiated.

There were certainly times when Henrik wondered how many
more obstacles could be placed in his path before he was finally
given the green light to move.

It would be wrong to suggest, at that stage, that Celtic
supporters were consumed by anxiety at the prospect of business
not being concluded. Given the status he now enjoys, it's
surprising to recall that most may not have been too sure what
to expect when new coach Jansen first expressed an interest in
signing Larsson.

Those cosmopolitan souls who watch every single World Cup
tie regardless of the teams involved may just have remembered
the promising youngster who had flourished briefly at the finals
in the USA three years earlier.

They may also have wondered what happened to the

dreadlocked star who had fallen out of favour at Feyenoord.

However much they did or didn't know about the 25-year-old, it's fair to say that by the time he eventually arrived at Celtic Park there was no major hype to live up to. Bunting had not been hung up and there were no street parties in Glasgow's East End to celebrate his signing.

Two years earlier, with supporters desperate for new heroes, the equally little-known German Andreas Thom had arrived from Bayer Leverkusen to a hero's welcome. But he failed to set the heather on fire during his time in Scotland.

Ironically, Larsson's signing effectively signalled the end of the road at Celtic Park for the under-achieving Thom who returned to his homeland before that momentous season had reached its climax.

However, for Larsson, thoroughly disillusioned by the way he was being treated in Rotterdam, Celtic's interest signalled a rebirth for a career that had been going nowhere – although the much delayed move might just as easily have ended with him killing it completely.

It was an unnecessarily protracted affair and one from which the Dutch giants emerged with little credit.

Once Jansen had been made aware that Larsson had a clause in his contract giving him the right to leave Holland if a foreign club were willing to pay a fee of £650,000 (the asking price for any interested Dutch club was a prohibitive £1.8m), the wheels were set in motion.

The bid was consequently made by Celtic. Although Larsson's contract had two years to run the transfer should have been perfectly straightforward. It was to prove anything but.

On July 12, several days after that bid had been lodged, Larsson said: "Celtic is the club I want to join and I have told Feyenoord I do not want to stay here. They cannot stop me."

It seemed, though, that events elsewhere were conspiring to block his bolt for freedom. A scheduled first trip to Scotland for a look round the Parkhead stadium had to be cancelled due to a British Airways strike which left Henrik stranded in Rotterdam airport.

Feyenoord, sensing too late that a major asset was about to be ripped from their hands, tried to ask for a higher fee, offering

32

Larsson £600,000 if they could lever £1.8m from Celtic.

To his credit the Swede refused to countenance the idea, insisting instead his case should be heard by an independent tribunal.

He said: "I will never return to Feyenoord. I'm devastated by the dirty games and all the rubbish thrown at me in the courts.

"It is all about money these days. There is no respect for the player and I will keep on fighting. If necessary I will go back to Sweden and play for an amateur team."

A frustrated Larsson broke down in tears on July 16 when the Dutch soccer tribunal ruled they needed more time to study the details of his appeal.

At that stage he had already opened preliminary talks with his former club Helsingborgs and was seriously contemplating a return there if the ruling went in Feyenoord's favour.

Hans Linae, a Swedish journalist and friend, recalled: "I remember Henrik making contact with Helsingborgs, telling them if he didn't sign for Celtic he would return.

"However, that would have provided him with another problem. He spoke of playing as an amateur in Sweden because he still had two years of his contract left to run.

"In our country, however, a player who has been a professional must wait one year before he can be reinstated as an amateur. Henrik would have put himself out of football.

"He told me later it was a very close thing. He was only a week or so from walking away from Feyenoord completely."

Meanwhile, Larsson's agent Rob Jansen kept the faith, saying: "Henrik is not happy and has his heart set on a move to Celtic.

"He knows he can play a major role in Wim Jansen's new set-up and I am sure that is where he will finish up."

Later, Henrik admitted: "It wasn't my ambition to go back to Sweden but I wanted to leave Holland. I was very unhappy for my last 18 months at Feyenoord.

"Different things happened and I don't want to go into it but the people responsible know who they are.

"Helsingborgs made me a very good offer but I told them that if another club came in for me I would prefer to play abroad because I was only 25."

The saga continued to drag on, however. Coach Haan made

Larsson join in the gruelling running sessions in the mornings but banned him from taking part with his team-mates in the afternoon bounce games.

Eventually, Henrik had had enough. On July 17 he refused to train with his team-mates and vowed never again to pull on a jersey for Feyenoord.

Four days later he received the news he had been privately dreading might never come when the Dutch FA's tribunal met at Zeist, ruled his contract was legitimate and declared he was free to become a Celtic player.

Personal terms hadn't even been discussed at that stage but a relieved Larsson insisted: "It's looking good. I now know what I'm going to do and that certainly means signing for Celtic."

After tying up a few loose ends in Rotterdam he touched down at Glasgow Airport on July 25 and grinned: "I am relaxed now that it is over. There was a lot of trouble over my contract but I knew I would win in the end.

"I had doubts if I would ever be able to come to Scotland because of all this but my agent kept telling me that Celtic's interest remained strong.

"That was very important to me. Other clubs said they were interested but only Celtic were strong enough to make me a concrete offer. I hope I can bring a lot to them.

"I was impressed by the way Pierre van Hooijdonk improved after coming here from NAC Breda. He was a good player in Holland but not as good as he is now. I also hope to improve my game.

"I am here because it is a big club which is well known all over Europe. Wim Jansen won the league immediately after taking over at Feyenoord and that is all the proof I need of his ability.

"There are no problems with my contract here – and if I'm successful I won't be asking for more money."

He laughed at that final remark – a reference to the "little problems" experienced by erstwhile heroes Paolo di Canio, Jorge Cadete and van Hooijdonk.

Before long Henrik wasn't just successful, he was indispensable. And lessons having been learned the hard way at Parkhead, his deal would be significantly improved and extended twice in the next four years.

At the time, though, Henrik was content to bed himself gently into the surroundings in the East End of Glasgow. The explosion would come later.

His first dozen matches yielded the – for him – paltry total of just five goals and it was during his introduction to the Scottish game that he became the victim of a crime which could never be perpetrated now. Less than a week after signing for Celtic, Larsson had his Visa card defrauded by petty thief Thomas McGowan.

It's as good an indication as any of the fact Henrik hadn't yet begun to ascend to the iconic status he now enjoys in this country that the 22-year-old McGowan, in spite of being white and not sporting dreadlocks, was able to use the card 25 times between August 1 and August 6 before being caught.

He bought designer clothes, jewellery and CDs as well as – more mundanely – razors, cigarettes and pet food from such outlets as Woolworths and Sainsburys.

McGowan, from Viewpark, Lanarkshire, admitted resetting stolen cards from Henrik and his wife and running up a bill of £1907.60.

Ironically, his case came to court on the weekend Larsson was presented with the PFA's Player of the Year award for 1999.

Sheriff Lewis Cameron had earlier said: "McGowan seems to have persuaded a large number of people that he was Henrik Larsson. Let's see what he looks like – we want a personal appearance."

A sheepish McGowan said: "I did not actually know who Henrik Larsson was at the time as he was not so famous then."

The Swede, meanwhile, was preoccupied with other problems, namely finding a home for himself and his new family, son Jordan – named after basketball superstar Michael – who was born just six weeks before the move.

Fortunately, while he trained and got to know his new team-mates, Magdalena was able to go house-hunting with Jansen's wife Cobi.

Henrik was also missing his dog who had been left behind in Holland. At the time he explained: "He's a Rhodesian Ridgeback and is a beautiful beast. It's easy to give away cats but dogs are different, they have their own character. It's very sad. Now I need to wait six months while he goes through quarantine. It's crazy. We also had a horse that belonged to Magdalena but I've told her we'll buy a new one in Scotland."

The Larssons soon found the home they were looking for in Bothwell and, domestic happiness having been established, Henrik set about making himself a legend.

His first Celtic goal came at Tynecastle – but not against Hearts. Henrik notched the second in a 7-0 demolition of Berwick Rangers in the Coca-Cola Cup after the tie had been switched from Shielfield Park to accomodate the travelling Celtic support.

Oddly, in view of what was to come, the first time Larsson found the net in Europe wearing the Hoops it was an own goal in a quite remarkable match.

It was a UEFA Cup qualifying tie against Tirol Innsbruck at Parkhead on August 27. Celtic had lost the first leg in Austria 2-1 but the return proved to be the club's biggest roller-coaster ride since the 5-4 win over Partizan Belgrade eight years earlier.

Simon Donnelly and Thom had given Celtic a 2-1 lead when Larsson diverted a cross from Christian Mayrleb past Jonathan Gould for Tirol's second equaliser.

Henrik atoned by winning a penalty, which Donnelly converted, then laid on a fourth for Craig Burley. But the Austrians made it 4-3 in the 82nd minute and with just two minutes left Celtic looked dead and buried.

Yet they refused to give in and sheer guts took them through with last-gasp goals from Morten Wieghorst and, in injury time, Burley (from another Larsson assist).

Some fans in the 47,000 crowd (how times have changed) had left after the visitors' third goal, an act that clearly baffled Henrik.

He said later: "They must understand you can't stop believing in the team or yourself.

"I'm sure the supporters regretted their actions when they reached their cars and heard the final score.

"My second-half performance was the best I've played for Celtic but I'm always confident of taking on and beating defenders if I get the ball. I'm also closer to match fitness. You must realise I hadn't played since May before I came to Glasgow."

He also admitted he feared he'd been cast as the villain of the piece again, so soon after his debut blunder against Hibs, and that his own goal would prove decisive.

Larsson said: "I was very frustrated. I started with an assist against Hibs that made Chic Charnley's winning goal on the first day of the season and after I scored in my own net I could see the headlines again.

"When Malky Mackay lost possession and the ball came across I tried to strike it with the outside of my foot to send it out for a corner, but only managed to put it into the corner of our net. I couldn't have done it again if I'd tried.

"I've never played in a game like that but the team wanted to win and so did I."

Celtic were unlucky to be eliminated by Liverpool on the away goals rule in the UEFA Cup first round proper but Jansen's side were growing in confidence by the week.

It wasn't all wine and roses, of course. A well-publicised training ground bust-up with team-mate Tosh McKinlay saw the Swede head-butted and nursing a black eye. The incident was soon forgotten by both players but McKinlay, who played for Scotland at the following summer's World Cup Finals, would never start a match under Wim again.

Meanwhile, Henrik's irresistible rise continued. If an omen was needed it arrived on September 22 when he grabbed both goals in the 2-0 home win over Aberdeen to mark his 26th birthday.

Larsson's first trophy in Scotland was, appropriately enough, picked up on St Andrew's Day when he scored the second goal in the 3-0 Coca-Cola Cup Final win over Tommy McLean's Dundee United.

However, it was his 19th and final goal of the season – amazingly a figure he equalled by November 12 last season – that figures prominently in the memory of most fans.

It came on May 9 on the final day of the season against St Johnstone at a packed Parkhead when a win would guarantee an end to Rangers' quest for a record 10 SPL championships in a row.

Celtic, understandably given the circumstances, started edgily and it took a goal right out of the Swede's top drawer – a curling right-footer from the far corner of the penalty area – to settle both players and supporters on that sun-drenched afternoon.

Harald Brattbakk, who suffered by comparison with his Scandinavian partner, picks that strike as Henrik's best.

The much-derided Norwegian, who scored the late clincher in a 2-0 win, said: "Without hesitation I would pick the goal Henrik scored that day as his most important and memorable for the club.

"He has hit many more since then but that one sticks in the mind because it was such a significant day for everybody.

"Henrik's strength and overall ability are awesome. It is really difficult to pick out any one thing because his entire game is strong. He can shoot, head, pass and score: what more do you want?"

Regi Blinker, a team-mate at Feyenoord as well as Celtic, also still rates it his favourite Henrik goal.

He said: "It was significant, not only because it helped win the title but it was one of those days when we didn't know if things were going to happen for us.

"But Henrik picked the ball up, buried it in the net and the nerves were more or less gone – it was so typical of him. I know that goal meant a lot to him as well as to the club and the fans.

"For me, Henrik's main strength is his all-round ability. But what people do not know is that he is a great learner – and he's still learning. Over the last year he has picked up much more to add to his game. His ability is better since coming to Celtic."

And so say all of us. As for Henrik, he said: "The Celtic fans had been in agony for nine years and we loved winning them the title."

Jansen would resign just 48 hours later, claiming he couldn't work with general manager Jock Brown. But even that blow couldn't halt the head of steam hotshot Henrik had started to build up.

However, there is no doubt Larsson has a special place in his personal Hall of Fame for the genius who rescued him from his Feyenoord misery.

Even if he hadn't been the coach who ended Rangers' quest for

10-in-a-row, Wim Jansen would have a special place in the hearts of Celtic fans just for being the man who brought Henrik to Parkhead.

It was, in fact, the second time the Dutchman had signed him, having taken him to Feyenoord from Helsingborgs in 1993.

But modest to a fault, Wim admits there was a huge stroke of luck involved when it came to spotting the future superstar first time round.

He said: "Sometimes it's hard to pick the right player for your side, and when I went to watch Henrik at Helsingborgs, he wasn't in my plans at all. I had gone to look at another striker who had been reccommended to me.

"However, Henrik was the most impressive player on the field. He had all the technical quality you could ask for.

"What I liked about him then is what I like about him now. He knew instinctively what to do without being told by anyone.

"He hadn't been capped by Sweden in those days – not for the full team at any rate – but he was already a clever player. Henrik was good in the air and he had quick feet. That made my decision easy.

"My initial target was forgotten and when I went back to Holland I told them Henrik was the man we needed to sign. As soon as I saw him I liked his style."

Like all great coaches, Jansen has total recall when it comes to football and the memory of what Larsson could do in the right surroundings never left him.

Which is why when he received the fateful call from Marcel van der Kram revealing Larsson's dissatisfaction in Rotterdam and his availability at a knockdown price Wim had no hesitation in making the move that would have such an enormous impact on the Scottish game.

He said: "As soon as I was appointed coach of Celtic I tried to sign Henrik. Obviously, after working with him I knew exactly how good he was but his qualities weren't coming out at that time at Feyenoord.

"They were forced to sell him because he had negotiated his contract well. I knew about his get-out clause but the most important thing all along was that we wanted him to play for us. I had a great feeling he would do very well for Celtic if he moved to Scotland and fortunately that's exactly what happened.

"I don't know what the appropriate transfer fee would be for him nowadays, that's very hard to say. But there's no doubt he has given value for money to Celtic.

"When you win a championship you win it as a team and everyone who is in the team is important. But the three key signings we made that season were undoubtedly Henrik, Craig Burley and Paul Lambert. They gave us the quality we needed while always playing for the team and not themselves.

"Of course, Henrik did very well in that first term when we won the title and the League Cup. But even then I knew he needed another striker to play off and to complement him.

"That was important to me and I tried to sign another one but at that time the club was not of a mind to buy the players I was looking at.

"I wanted to partner him with somebody of Chris Sutton's calibre because I knew Henrik would do better if he had someone like that alongside him. I think everyone saw that last season.

"He is doing very well now, going from strength to strength, and I am very pleased for him."

Like every other football addict, and especially those who have worked with Larsson, Jansen was concerned about the after-effects of the double fracture suffered in Lyon.

Wim admitted: "When a player has an injury as serious as that it's not easy to come back and be as effective as you used to be.

"However, I went to see him at Euro 2000 in one of his first matches after the broken leg. He scored an outstanding goal against Italy, whose defence was probably the best in the tournament.

"I was surprised he did so well but after that I knew for sure he would come back strongly."

Although Jansen's own spell at Parkhead was cut short following his well-publicised series of bust-ups with Jock Brown, he never at any time believed Larsson would quit the club he has grown to love.

He said: "Henrik has been linked with moves to other teams but he loves being with Celtic and that's crucial.

"If a person like him feels comfortable and wanted at a club, then he'll be happy. I've heard he's spoken about going back to Sweden when his latest contract expires in 2004 but that will be his decision and no one else's. Henrik knows what to do during a match and he knows what to do with his career. I found him very easy to work with.

"You never have to worry about him because he always knows the right things to do. When you're at training you don't need to tell him if he needs to work harder on one particular aspect of his game because he'll realise that himself. He's a real professional.

"The next few years should see Henrik at his absolute peak. I certainly hope so both for him and for Celtic."

# four season 97-98

FEW people in Scotland know Henrik Larsson better than Celtic legend Murdo MacLeod.

Working as assistant manager to Wim Jansen in season 1997-98, MacLeod built up a special relationship with the striker that stretched way beyond the boundaries of the dressing-room. The bond continues to this day, the duo regularly enjoying a game of golf or a meal together.

The pair played a significant role in wrestling the title from Rangers that season as a tremendous spirit drove the Celts squad to stop their bitter rivals claiming 10-in-a-row.

MacLeod was originally appointed by former owner Fergus McCann as reserve team boss during that summer as the long and tiring search for a successor to Tommy Burns began.

Jansen, a Dutch legend, was eventually unveiled but his appointment was met with ridicule. He was a relative unknown in this country and far from the sexy name the fans expected after the club was strongly linked with former England manager Bobby Robson, in charge of Barcelona at that time.

However, a deal couldn't be struck to bring Robson to

Parkhead and Jansen was handed the reins – hailed as a panic measure at the time.

MacLeod helped the new gaffer out during their pre-season camp at Arnhem in Holland and the pair hit it off so well that he was promoted within a fortnight to Wim's right-hand man.

The pair, along with Davie Hay, worked night and day to strengthen the squad and Larsson, a player Jansen knew well from his days in Holland with Feyenoord, was top of their list.

After a court case to release him from his contract, Larsson arrived at Celtic Park a few days before the start of the season. However, his debut hardly went to plan as Henrik's mistake at Easter Road handed Hibs victory in the opening league game of the season.

Another defeat followed at home to Dunfermline and the roof looked like it was going to cave in. Who was this guy Jansen? Why was he wasting money buying duds like Larsson?

But MacLeod never had any fears. And despite Henrik's unimpressive start the Scot knew the club had a diamond would polish up into a fabulous gem given time.

MacLeod, who now runs a successful restaurant, said: "I remember Henrik having a bad start in his debut when he came off the bench against Hibs and gave away possession to Chic Charnley, who rattled the ball into the net for the winner. It was the first match of the season and the last thing we needed was a defeat.

"A lot of attention focussed on Henrik because of that mistake but he tried to make a joke of it by saying things could only get better – and they did.

"But it also helped Charnley's profile step up a level and he wound up being tipped for a Scotland call-up after that goal.

"Chic was delighted about his strike and kept shouting over to our bench to ask if we had seen it. Maybe he was trying to get Wim to sign him, I'm not sure!

"However, after that Henrik just worked away and didn't let the pressure get to him. He trained hard the next day, as he had just joined us so missed our pre-season. He also worked tirelessly on his shooting and used to get very angry with himself if he failed to hit the target.

"His physique is incredible and yet when he first joined the

44

club he never bothered going into the gym for any serious weight training. He must have had a natural muscular build. Later in the season he did go to the gym to do a bit and still does now. He is as solid as a rock and if you try to brush him off the ball you just bounce off.

"I often faced him in training games and he was an absolute nightmare to play against. I'd get the ball, and he'd be about 15 yards away and I'd think I had time to take a touch. But as soon as that touch was taken he'd be on top of me before I knew it, closing me down and not letting me make a pass. To be fair, he was like that with all of the players.

"The reason he gets to you so quickly is that he can read the game well. He's one of the best I have ever worked with for reading situations. He just has this incredible knack of knowing when you are going to take a touch and the direction you will take it in. He wins so many balls from defenders that way.

"He also liked to get wired in during the training games and even though I was the assistant manager he never hesitated to have a kick at me if he thought it was the right thing to do at that moment."

Despite Larsson now being hailed as one of Europe's outstanding strikers, he – and Celtic – were unsure of his best position when he arrived at the club. Some thought it was as an attacking left sided midfielder, others suggested it was in the hole behind the front-men. But everyone worked hard to find a solution and produced one of the game's most prized assets.

MacLeod puts that down to the Swede's work-rate and professionalism and said: "The first thing I noticed about Henrik was his attitude, it was first class. I remember we used to play wee games at training and he would always be desperate to win. He hates losing and that's one of the reasons he is such a tremendous player.

"But we weren't sure if he was an out and out striker, the man to lead the line. Henrik wasn't really sure either and at that time he preferred to be just off the hitmen linking up in most areas of the pitch. But over the last couple of years, as we all know, he is now the main striker and his ability has enabled him to score with his right foot, his left and with headers.

"His first touch is also outstanding and I'm sure most

footballers would love to have Henrik's touch and control. I suppose the best way to put it is that he is the complete striker.

"He was instrumental in our championship success that season and, although he's scored more goals since, Henrik still led the team up front and you can't put a value on that.

"We had Paul Lambert and Craig Burley in the middle, Alan Stubbs and Marc Rieper in the heart of the defence and the likes of Jackie McNamara out on the right. They all knew what to do when they went out onto the pitch and were all capable of being leaders on the pitch when it was needed. In fact we had so many consistent performers we must have had at least four or five players in the running for the Player of the Year awards.

"Ultimately though Henrik was the man we relied on to put the ball in the net and that will always grab the headlines. His strike on the final day of the season against St Johnstone was priceless.

"There was great pressure on us, as we had to win to be sure of the title. On occasions like that you need someone like Henrik and he set us on our way with a magnificent goal after two minutes when he drilled past Alan Main from about 25 yards.

"The other goal I remember him for was also against St Johnstone, this time in Perth, and he played the biggest one-two I've ever seen. Henrik played the ball out wide to Donnelly, who then crossed for Larsson at the edge of the box and he scored with a fantastic diving header. It really was an unbelievable goal and a vitally important one for us as it was our first win in the league and we took off from there."

The £650,000 transfer fee Celtic paid to land Larsson now seems totally ridiculous and MacLeod admits Celtic would have been prepared to pay four times as much if the get-out clause was not written into the striker's contract.

He said: "When you look now at the fee we paid for Larsson it has to be one of the steals of the century. Wim was aware he had a clause in his contract to leave Feyenoord for that amount, but even without that Wim would still have pursued him and would have paid £2.5million without thinking twice.

"Henrik was always his number one target and we discussed other players such as Paul Lambert coming in and trying to bring John Collins back to the club. But Wim wanted to concentrate on Henrik. He would have been our first signing had there not been the problems with the courtcase."

MacLeod's business in Croftamie is thriving, he is a popular radio and television pundit as well as a columnist with the Daily Record, but there are times he still feels cheated that he didn't get the chance to stay in his management longer than one season.

The relationship between Jansen and his superiors broke down and the Dutchman couldn't take the political interference any more. He quit 48 hours after Celtic clinched the title to move back to Rotterdam and hasn't worked full-time in the game since.

MacLeod was keen to replace Jansen and build on the foundations but always felt he had next to no chance and the only realistic option would be to follow Jansen out the door. He did and he, too, hasn't been in full-time football employment since, although both have turned down attractive offers to work together again.

Murdo often wonders what might have been if he hadn't parted company with the club, especially working with Henrik as his career hit new heights.

MacLeod said: "I would love to have been able to work with Henrik for longer and it would be nice to still be in there beside him and the other boys today. But the situation came to an end under bad circumstances and we all felt a bit let down and cheated because we weren't allowed to build on our success.

"I know Henrik was annoyed and disappointed with it all as he built up a good relationship with Wim and wanted to keep working with him. But being the good professional he is he just got on with things rather than mump and moan, which is the way Wim and myself wanted it to be anyway.

"Under new management the following seasons Henrik played just as hard for Jozef Venglos and John Barnes as he would have if we were still in charge.

"Still we had a good thing going at that time and I really felt we could go on to build a bright new era in the Celtic's history.

"We had a new team coming together. Apart from Henrik, Marc Rieper, Craig Burley, Stephane Mahe and Jonathan Gould were all new to the club and Paul Lambert was on his way from

Borussia Dortmund, arriving in November. So the spirit was building up nicely and despite the fact we lost our opening two league games of the season, we still felt we had the ability and belief in the squad to win the title and stop Rangers from making it 10-in-a-row.

"Of course, we managed to do it. And although winning three points on a Saturday is the main reason for that, another reason was the team spirit we built, it was second to none.

"The boys enjoyed a game of golf together and would have a meal and couple of drinks afterwards. Henrik liked the game and we still play together often. I think his handicap is 14 and I love taking him on because he has still to beat me. Considering he is just new to golf his handicap is terrific and it makes you wonder if there is anything he isn't good at.

"The players wanted to have the golf days and it was their idea to get them started, especially the foreign boys.

"Henrik enjoys getting away from the pressures of football but when we are out together he is just a normal guy, someone you would meet at the local pub.

"He is down to earth, likes talking about football and about his family. They are very important to him and he would do anything for his wife Magdalena and son Jordan to make them happy.

"He's not the type of guy who is off clubbing every second night. The only time I've known him to go out was on organised team nights, other than that he'd be with the family, spending time at home or on a quiet night out.

"I wish him all the best because he deserves it. He is a credit to himself, his family and Celtic Football Club."

Another man who can count himself as one of Henrik's closest friends is Danish defender Rieper.

When the big centre-back walked into the Celtic dressing-room in season 1997-98 he knew they had a chance of winning the title that season because there was a certain striker at the club with the dreadlocks and white headband.

Rieper arrived from West Ham in a complicated £1.5million deal that seemed to take an eternity to go through. But when he finally managed to get up to Glasgow his presence in the side was just as crucial as that of his fellow Scandanavian.

Rieper settled in quickly and, just as importantly, helped £3.5million defensive partner Alan Stubbs play like his true self after a difficult first season at the club under Tommy Burns when Rangers won nine-in-a-row to equal Celtic's proud record.

Stubbs found it hard to cope with the pressure on and off the park playing for one half of the Old Firm and it looked as though his career at Parkhead would end in failure. But Rieper's presence brought solidity to the back-line with his no-nonsense style, allowing Stubbs to relax and concentrate on reading the game and bringing the ball out of defence.

Celtic had now completed their back four of Tom Boyd, Rieper, Stubbs and Mahe, the backbone on which their championship success of that season was built on.

Once the defence was stable and efficient, it was left for Larsson to do his stuff at the other end, and Rieper was delighted to see him respond.

In fact, Marc, now assistant head coach of Danish side Aarhus, has already made moves to take Larsson to Denmark and sign for his club. In his first meeting with the club president, Rieper identified Henrik as the man to make it happen for his new team and revealed the moves behind the scenes to land him.

He said: "I would love to have Henrik here with me and have discussed it with the President but we are a little bit skint just now so it might not be possible. In fact, we are about £24.9m short of the fee, so unless Celtic would let him go for £100,000 we will have to forget about it! But seriously, it would be nice to have him here not just for his ability on the park but his professionalism off the pitch. He has been, and will continue to be, a great servant to Celtic and Scottish football.

"Before I arrived at Parkhead I had played against Henrik at club level and international level and he always impressed me. Even though I was much bigger and stronger than him he was never afraid. He would get stuck in, no matter the size of his opponent and always made life very difficult.

"I suppose knowing he was already at Celtic helped to make up my mind about joining the club. I knew we would have a chance of being successful with Henrik in the team and that's the way it turned out. We won the league and the Coca-Cola Cup and Henrik played a big part.

"We always knew that if we could keep it tight at the back we would have a chance of collecting the three points with Henrik up front. You've no idea how comforting it is to have a player of that quality in the team. The only downside is that he spoils you and you are unlikely to ever play with anyone else like him.

"I don't really have one favourite memory of him from our time together at Celtic. It's not like he is dead or something and I have one thing to remember him by. I can still see him on television and I enjoy watching the Celtic games and seeing him continue to help the team to win games.

"I loved watching the team win the Treble and even though I wasn't at the club I still felt a part of it. That's what Celtic does to you, you never really leave even though you are not there in person any more. Henrik will feel the same when his time comes to leave because he is loyal person, honest and reliable.

"You know when he says something or tells you something that it is truth. That, for me, is just as important as being able to put the ball in the net and it is a quality not everyone in life has."

Rieper and Larsson became very close off the park and still share a special relationship. They are often in contact by telephone as Henrik keeps Marc up to date with the goings-on at Celtic.

And Rieper would probably still be lining up with his pal had a toe injury not cruelly ended his career at the age of 31.

Many feared Larsson's playing days were also over when he broke his leg against Lyon but the Swede has bounced back in style.

During Henrik's rehabilitation, Rieper had been promoted to part of the Celtic backroom team along with Kenny Dalglish and Tommy Burns after John Barnes and Eric Black were dismissed.

Rieper was a rock for the Swedish striker at that time as he helped to bring him on and encourage him back to full fitness.

Marc recalled: "When the injury happened I have to be honest and say I wondered what Henrik would be like when he came back. I had no doubts he would play football again for Celtic but you had to wonder what kind of performances would he be able to produce.

"He was so keen to return and prove to himself and everyone as quickly as possible that he was in good shape. And he did, didn't he? In fact, he has come back better than ever and I am absolutely delighted for him. Sometimes I'd watch Henrik and think he should be taking a bit easier when he was trying to come back and I think the medical staff had to rein him in a little bit. Still, it has all worked out so well in the end for him and the club.

"But although his ability as a football player will never be in question I have to tell you he struggles at golf. I love playing against him because I always beat him, although I'm sure if you talked to Henrik he would tell you he beats me all the time. Honestly, don't believe him!"

Despite their close friendship, Rieper has no idea what the future holds for Larsson when he hangs up his boots. The big Dane suspects he might want to get involved coaching kids and Rieper believes he would be fantastic at bringing on young strikers.

He said: "Near the end of my career I always insisted I would never become a manager and get into the day-to-day side of running a football club. Look at me now though, I am an assistant manager of one of Denmark's biggest outfits.

"I have a feeling Henrik will not want to follow in my footsteps and would prefer to coach youths. I think that would be perfect for him as he would be a tremendous asset to a club. Can you honestly think of a better person or footballer to teach your kids?

"He will do his best to show them how to control a ball and then score with it. But he will also teach them good habits to get them through life. I like that kind of thing and would trust him to look after my kids, that's what I think of him.

"Maybe, though, he will end up wanting to become a manager. Football is like a drug in many ways and you might think it will be easy to walk away from it, but it is not. We will just have to wait and see. Maybe then I'll be able to get Henrik to Aarhus on a Bosman!"

One young man who learned his trade under the watchful eye of Larsson was Simon Donnelly. The Celtic youth product can proudly boast the honour of being Henrik's first regular striking partner in the hoops and admits he has yet to meet the Swede's equal.

Donnelly, who left for Sheffield Wednesday in 1999, grinned: "That double-winning season was something of a blur and it all seems so long ago now. But I remember enough to know Henrik is easily the best striker I've ever played with, and he's improved further since I was there.

"It's funny to think that when he first arrived no-one had these great expectations. Given his price tag at that time, we couldn't have imagined what he'd go on to achieve or what he'd be worth in the current transfer market.

"We played together until Harald Brattbakk arrived at the end of November and scored 25 goals between us before Christmas.

"I felt lucky to have partnered him. Henrik was great to work off due to his non-stop movement but that didn't happen all by itself.

"He and Paolo di Canio are the two hardest-working guys I've ever seen at training and both reaped the benefit of that graft where it matters, on the park.

"Henrik keeps himself to himself, which is maybe the best way to deal with things: you never read about his private life in the papers.

"I must say, though, that every time I've gone back to Parkhead he's always taken the time to have a chat and ask how I'm getting on. He is a good friend."

The camaraderie generated in the double winners' dressing room played a huge part in their success. With Jansen forced to sign so many new players in such a short space of time the process of bonding had to be speeded up.

Burley, Stubbs and Tom Boyd were the chief organisers of regular first-team squad days out, whether it was go-karting, paintball or just a meal and a drink together.

This fostered an all-for-one spirit that took them all the way to the title – and Henrik enjoyed being part of the booze brothers as much as anyone.

Simon revealed: "It was a different culture to what he had been used to and it took him a bit of time to get to know all the boys. But those days out definitely helped.

"You won't find any member of that squad who has a bad

word to say about Henrik. He's such an easy-going guy."

Generosity is another quality Donnelly reckons Larsson can add to him impressive list – just take Brattbakk for example.

The Norwegian came to Parkhead with an impressive scoring record for Rosenborg, particularly in Champions League matches, but never truly adapted to the hurly burly of the Scottish game.

Forwards though, like keepers, tend to stick together in times of crisis and Henrik did all he could to boost his pal's confidence.

Donnelly said: "I remember one home match against St Johnstone the following season that sums Henrik up.

"Harald was playing alongside him at the time and was going through a particularly sticky spell with goals hard to come by.

"You always feel for a fellow striker in that situation because we all struggle at some stage, although Henrik doesn't seem to suffer too often these days.

"Anyway, that night Henrik had set up a few chances for Harald. Henrik had scored once and Harald twice and we were 4-0 up with only minutes remaining.

"Then Henrik was sent clear, took the ball round Alan Main... and rolled it into Harald's path for a tap-in when he could easily have scored himself after doing the spadework.

"You could tell he felt for Harald and was genuinely happy that he helped him get his hat-trick after he had come in for some stick. That's the sign of a good player. There was definitely an element there of Henrik doing his pal a turn.

"He genuinely doesn't care who scores, although it's probably easier to be unselfish when you bag as many as he does."

It may be hard to imagine, and opposing SPL defenders will certainly hope it isn't the case, but Sid is convinced Larsson is still getting better.

He said: "I watched him on TV at the start of this season and, if it's possible, I think he may have moved up yet another gear. His all-round play against Manchester United at Old Trafford in Ryan Giggs' testimonial was phenomenal. He didn't score in Celtic's 4-3 win but was unbelievable, particularly when you consider he was up against Jaap Stam.

"Confidence is probably the most important factor in a striker's make-up and you can tell Henrik has bags of it. He looks so sharp, every bit like a guy who's just grabbed over 50 goals in a season.

"He's trying all sorts of things you would only ever attempt when you feel at the top of your game and long may it continue."

Brattbakk himself also has fond memories of his days playing alongside one of Celtic's finest-ever strikers.

He arrived in Glasgow in December 1997 sporting glasses and manners good enough for royalty – not exactly what you would expect from a man tipped to fire Celtic to glory.

After a four month search when targets such as Barcelona's Juan Antonio Pizzi and Karl-Heinz Riedle from Borussia Dortmund failed to be landed, Brattbakk was identified as the man to partner Larsson. Norwegian side Rosenborg received a £2million transfer fee and the frontman strolled into Celtic Park boasting an impressive CV including goals in the Champions League.

But despite his undeniable strike-rate, his ability and bottle were questioned from day one by people in his native country and it wasn't long before the Scots were whispering in agreement.

Brattbakk felt the strain and was never fully accepted by the Celtic fans. He badly wanted to be a success and was desperate to match the plaudits his strike partner Henrik Larsson was getting. Henrik could do no wrong, Harald could do no right.

The Norwegian would watch with envious eyes as his team-mates ripped defences apart week-in, week-out and wonder what he could do to compete with them. But the harder he tried, the worse it became. However, Brattbakk didn't grudge Larsson one ounce of his success, even though he wanted it all for himself.

Now back banging in goals for fun with Rosenborg, he said: "I have nothing but admiration for Henrik Larsson. In many ways it is not easy to be successful at Celtic because there is so much pressure on you to do well every week for 90 minutes. There is no hiding place out there and it is pretty much a case of sink or swim.

"At times, I found the pressure difficult to cope with and it didn't help when I was out on the pitch. Sometimes I would maybe be nervous and that meant I wasn't properly relaxed.

"Henrik had no such trouble. He could cope with everything

and had this supreme quality of not letting things get to him. If he missed a chance he would just make sure he put the next one in the net. He wouldn't hide or go into a shell.

"Part of that must have been the fact the supporters were right behind him. He could do no wrong because he was Henrik Larsson, the man they trusted to win them games.

"The Celtic fans were right to treat him that way because he is an exceptional player, the best I have ever played with in my entire career without one bit of doubt in my mind. He was unselfish and would prefer to let others score before himself – not many strikers have that attitude.

"Sometimes though I just wished I could have changed places with him for a while. I'm not saying I was treated badly by the Celtic fans but it would have been nice to be treated like a hero for every minute of every match."

At least Brattbakk has the consolation of scoring on the day Celtic won the league in 1998 when he netted against St Johnstone in a 2-0 win after Larsson got the opening goal.

That is his most treasured memory in football and he said: "Henrik and I were strike partners and it was great for both to score on the most important day of the season.

"We had a chance to win the title at Dunfermline the week before but allowed them to equalise. It meant the league went right to the last game but it worked out great because we could win it in front of our fans.

"It was one big party and I loved every minute. To score that day was incredible, that one moment made my two years there worth it, every single second of the difficult times as well.

"We then had a party to celebrate and to be honest I can't remember much about it. I hardly had any energy left because it was a tiring day, mentally and physically but we all deserved it.

"We worked hard that season and the gold medal was the perfect reward. Nobody will ever be able to take that day away from me."

But it was very much downhill from then on for Brattbakk and he slipped down the pecking order for a place in the starting line-up as other strikers such as Mark Viduka and Lubo Moravcik arrived during Dr Venglos' time in charge. Mark Burchill also emerged about the same time.

The two foreign signings turned out to be highly successful, leaving Brattbakk in the stand more often than not. Things didn't change when Barnes took over in the summer of 1999 and the Norwegian was transferred during that season in a £700,000 move to Danish side FC Copenhagen.

He was sad and disappointed to leave but felt he had no choice. Harald said: "Oh yes, I would love to still be at Celtic. They are a very big club and it was my pleasure to have played for them.

"But I felt I wasn't getting a chance on a regular basis to show what I could do and I had to think about my future and investigate any possibilities. I had to go somewhere else.

"The chance to leave eventually came and I was sad. I wanted to play for Celtic, I wanted to play beside Henrik every week. He tried to help me and would offer advice, especially on the pitch. Off the pitch, though, players mostly look after themselves and will think about doing what is best for them.

"I have no complaints about that. Football is a team game, I know that. But I also know that if you try too hard for other people you might end up forgetting about yourself and that is not right. You have to be the priority in your own mind and I will always take care of myself first of all."

At least Brattbakk got a bit of revenge when he scored twice against his old club for Copenhagen during Martin O'Neill's first pre-season game in charge, albeit against the central defensive pairing of Olivier Tebily and Rafael Scheidt.

No-one would have thought back then that O'Neill would turn it all round and lead the club to the Treble. But Brattbakk was thrilled to see Celtic do so well and has been on the phone to congratulate Larsson and his other former team-mate Morten Wieghorst on their success.

He said: "I follow Celtic closely as they are very special to me. I keep in touch with Henrik and Morten and there are only good things to say about Celtic just now.

"Henrik enjoyed a fabulous season last year and wants to do it all over again. I don't know how he can possibly manage that but if anyone can, then it will be Henrik. I wish the club all the best for the future."

# five season 98-99

A TYPICAL argument between Old Firm fans is over who has had the greatest foreign player on their books. Followers of Rangers, of course, would go for Brian Laudrup. Those of the Hooped persuasion would plump for Henrik Larsson.

So who's better and who's best? Well, the Great Dane helped Rangers steam towards nine-in-a-row, an achievement that will be forever remembered in the history of the Ibrox club with his name beside others such as Andy Goram, Richard Gough, Ally McCoist, Stuart McCall and Ian Durrant.

Laudrup, who wore No.11, was as skilful a player as you'll ever see. He had defenders up and down the country bamboozled right from his competitive debut for Rangers with his sublime touch and control, ability to glide past players and score the occasional goal only extraordinary talents are capable of.

Brian was the undisputed King of the Premier League, collecting all sorts of personal awards as well as collective ones for the team during Walter Smith's era after he signed for the club from Fiorentina in a £2.2m deal in the summer of 1994.

Three seasons later Mr Larsson appeared on the scene on the

opposite side of the city but his introduction was far from impressive, starting with the nightmare debut against Hibs.

Gradually, though, Henrik's unmistakable talent shone through as he captured the hearts of all genuine football lovers. He followed in Laudrup's footsteps to be crowned the country's top player by the PFA and Scottish Football Writers' after a fantastic season under Jozef Venglos in 1998-99, despite Rangers winning the Treble. Even the Ibrox fans have applauded some of his skills, the way the Celtic crowd used to with Laudrup.

Brian too, has risen to his feet in admiration of the talented Swede when watching Celtic's games on television in his home in Denmark.

Now retired from the professional game and working as a summariser for Danish TV, Laudrup lavished praise on Larsson and still with a hint of a Scottish accent said: "I have watched Henrik closely since he arrived in Glasgow and he thoroughly deserved his awards from the 1998-99 season. He is superb.

"It is wrong for people not to recognise and fully appreciate how well he has performed. His goalscoring has been incredible and the people who say he has only managed to do it because he plays in an inferior league are talking rubbish. In fact, it is insulting to Henrik and to Scottish football.

"We are talking about a top player, a man who has done it regularly at the very highest level for Sweden, one of Europe's strongest footballing nations. He is the kind of player who can be the difference between two close sides. He can score out of nothing and the other sensational thing is that he does it in almost every game, whereas others might just turn it on in every third or fourth match.

"I'm sure any manager in the land would love to have Larsson. I know he would be my type if I coached a team and I'd move heaven and earth to get him as he is the type of player and person to build a team around.

"I don't know how much money I would pay for him, it would depend on my budget. But when I look around it seems nowadays you only have to be able to pass a ball 10 yards to be worth £6m. So Henrik must be worth £20m and it would be much more than that if he was two or three years younger.

"It is incredible to think of the money Celtic got him for.

People used to say I was a bargain at £2.2m. What does that make Henrik at £650,000? Unique, I guess.

"And I think he will get better. His game appears to have improved with Chris Sutton beside him and their understanding is bound to get better, which is bad news for the rest of Scotland.

"Last season was incredible for Henrik. I mean, come on, 53 goals. How can anyone criticise that? It is even more remarkable when you realise it all happened so soon after his leg break in Lyon. Yet people must have thought he'd never be the same, some may even have asked if he'd ever play for Celtic again.

"But I know Larsson must have been desperate to get back as soon as possible because he must feel proud when he pulls on a Celtic jersey and hears the fans chanting his name. I had that special relationship with the Rangers supporters and it is one of the best feelings in the world to know you are wanted and appreciated by people who care deeply about football.

"I will always have a special place in my heart for my time with Rangers, no matter what I do in the future. I know Henrik will be the same with Celtic and it is that kind of thing that makes Glasgow and the Old Firm so unique. It would only happen at a few other clubs around the world.

"If people are making comparisons between the two of us that is up to them. I was good for Rangers and I hope never to be forgotten, Henrik will be the same with Celtic. But as to who is the best foreigner to play in Scotland? I don't think that is a nice argument for me to get involved in because in some ways we are similar and in other ways we are totally different. All I will say is that the Rangers fans would favour me and the Celtic fans will favour Henrik. That is the best way for me to put it!

"But the good thing from both our points of view is that we are both Scandinavian and feel very proud to be held in such high esteem. It is a credit to Denmark and Sweden that we are regarded in this way."

Larsson has been criticised and accused of showing a lack of ambition for singing a new contract with Celtic and not asking away to test himself in England, Italy or Spain.

That kind of talk infuriates Laudrup. He, more than anyone, knows you shouldn't move on just for the sake of it. He went through hell in Italy as his private life was invaded and his family suffered awful verbal abuse because he couldn't live up to the high expectations of the demanding media and fans.

That's why he chose to move to Rangers, a place he would be appreciated and an environment where the Laudrups could get back to leading as normal a life as possible. They found that at their house in Helensburgh, so much so that they may return one day to set up home again.

The Ibrox legend said: "It is tremendous for Celtic that they managed to keep Henrik. In fact, the whole of Scottish football should be proud to have a player of his calibre wanting to stay, rather than moving on at the first opportunity.

"Other clubs will benefit from having him in the country and although they might not think that when he is scoring goals against them if they look at the bigger picture it is bound to attract players to Scotland if they know Henrik is there. They will think that if it is good enough for Larsson it must be good enough for them.

"But it is wrong to look at him staying as a negative thing. I respect and understand his decision because he is a family man and if they are settled that is the most important thing.

"Maybe if he was single and enjoyed nightclubbing and drinking he might fancy a career change with a new environment. But from what I know about him that is definitely not his style. He doesn't go in for that sort of thing, his family and enjoyment from the game are his two priorities. I was exactly the same and there's absolutely nothing wrong with being that way. He should be respected and congratulated for it.

"Anyway, people who go on about trying a different more competitive league don't fully understand what it is all about.

"Italy, England and Spain can sometimes not be as good as everyone thinks. I should know, I've been there and had some painful experiences. Believe me, feeling happy at your work and knowing your family is content means much more than the league you're in and the players you play with and against.

"However, I know the pressure Henrik must have been under to try something new and he deserves credit for sticking to his beliefs. I remember after my first season at Ibrox when we won the League and I won the Player of the Year awards, everyone had me moving on and wondering where I would like to try next.

"That wasn't for me. I was happy at Rangers and wanted to stay there to repay the faith shown in me by Walter Smith, David Murray, my team-mates and the supporters. Sure, I moved on but I stayed four years and they were without doubt the happiest of my career in football.

"When Henrik retires from the game he will have the same things to say, I'm positive about that."

While the argument over the finest foreigner to play for the Old Firm will rage on, former Celtic coach Eric Black is in no doubt who gets his vote.

Black himself was rated as a striker with the potential to go to the very top and stay there. He played in Sir Alex Ferguson's all-conquering Aberdeen side in the 1980s that ended the Old Firm's dominance and also lifted the European Cup Winners' Cup when Dons beat Real Madrid 2-1 in Gothenburg in 1983.

But, cruelly, a persistent back injury forced Eric to retire at the age of just 27, less than a year into his career with French side Metz. He then made a name for himself in the coaching world and landed a job in the SFA where he was tipped to be a natural successor to Scotland coach Craig Brown. But Celtic nipped in to steal his services in the summer of 1997 as Youth Development coach and he was eventually promoted a year later to be assistant head coach to Jozef Venglos, a job he kept when John Barnes took over a year later.

Black revelled in his role and got fantastic pleasure working with Larsson every day. He revealed: "I worked with him under Venglos and Barnes the following season, and from a coaching point of view there can be no complaints about Henrik.

"In fact, the game of football would be much better off if a few more professionals had his attitude and dedication.

"He is the ultimate pro and everything he does is geared towards performing for the team on match day. He is focused for every possibility and leaves nothing to chance in his preparation. And that is not just for himself, he does that for the good of the team, too.

"Henrik likes a bit of fun when the time is right and he has a great sense of humour. He loves the dressing-room banter and is never slow to get involved in a wind-up.

"But when it was the right time to concentrate completely on the match, he would be sitting down 15 minutes before kick-off with a towel over his head to shut himself off from everything and focus on the 90 minutes. Then he came to life on the field.

"It was just a pity we didn't win anything that season and had to watch Rangers sweep the board. But it says a lot for Henrik that he was still voted the best player in the country by everyone, even though we had no success as a team."

Black rates Larsson in the £20m bracket and knows that if the Bhoys gave any indication they'd be willing to sell him Europe's finest clubs would be breaking down the door.

He said: "You could put Henrik in any team, successful or unsuccessful, and he would still do well. Last season the amount of goals he scored was absolutely incredible.

"I know it is not as easy to put the ball in the net as Henrik makes it look. It takes a special talent, something you are probably born with but have to work hard to keep going.

"He is pure quality and has developed to a new level over the past two years. Don't get me wrong, he was very, very good when he arrived from Feyenoord in 1997 but I think he has improved and I'm sure he would tell you that himself.

"He has gained confidence along with his scoring achievements and putting the ball in the net is what strikers live for. Henrik certainly has that ability and it's hard to see him losing it.

"He is a top, top striker and could perform in any league in the world without a hint of a problem. I know people have suggested he only does well because Scotland isn't the most testing of leagues, but Henrik would score goals anywhere. He does it for Sweden against star defenders from other countries so nobody should be taken in by some of the comments.

"There is no way Celtic would consider letting him go and the fact they have just given him his new contract is proof. But if they did decide to sell they could ask up to £20m easily. Every club in the land would want him in their squad.

"I think he'll just continue to play for Celtic and keep scoring plenty of goals. He will never lose that skill, at least Celtic hope he never will. Rangers, though, might have a different opinion."

One man who can vouch for the striker's ability is ex-Bhoys keeper Stewart Kerr.

Not only did the keeper have to leave his beloved Celtic Park to secure first-team football but he also had to try and stop Henrik Larsson scoring EVERY DAY!

Only a move to Wigan for £250,000 relieved the stopper of his daily training duties where he admits he was often left humiliated as the Swede turned on his tricks.

Kerr said: "From day one Henrik was a dedicated trainer and would work as hard as he did on a Saturday. It wasn't easy for the likes of myself and the other goalies Jonathan Gould, Rab Douglas and Dmitri Kharine as he takes training so seriously.

"He is very hard on himself and is his own biggest critic. He would get very angry if he missed a chance, but I have to say that wasn't very often. If he didn't hit the net he would at least hit the target, forcing us to make a save.

"Many times Henrik embarrassed me during the one-on-one practice sessions. He was excellent at dinking the ball over you, sliding it low, taking it round you or even just blasting it.

"That was what was so tricky about him, you just never knew what he was going to do.

"The secret for us was to try and stand up for as long as possible, stay big. If you went down too quickly he would punish you. Yes, it was always a real test against Henrik and that is one thing I don't miss about being away from Celtic.

"During all my time at the club he was the sharpest finisher I ever played against. Mark Viduka was also very good and then there was Paolo di Canio who was also blessed with tremendous talent.

"But Paolo always tried to look for the perfect finish, whereas Henrik would just do what was necessary to put the ball in the back of the net. At the end of the day that is what football is all about – goals win prizes.

"He's the ultimate professional and a credit to himself and Celtic. Despite the success, such as winning the Golden Shoe last season he never let it go to his head. Some guys would get big-headed but Henrik has stayed the same, completely modest.

"He spends loads of time signing autographs for the kids at the stadium and sometimes during the school holidays might be there signing and posing for photographs for more than an hour. But he knows you need to do that to give the fans their moment of pleasure and he would never ever moan about it."

Kerr was sorry to leave Parkhead but knew it had to be done for the sake of his career. Now he has the chance to play first-team football every week with ambitious English Second Division side Wigan after falling down the pecking order under Martin O'Neill's regime.

Stewart feels he has left behind a club on the verge of some serious glory days and believes it is going to be very difficult for Rangers to catch Celtic, especially if Larsson stays fit and continues to produce the goods.

He said: "Henrik is a player of great importance to Celtic and no-one can underestimate what he does for the club and the dressing-room. He is a positive influence, whether he has his strip on or is wearing his everyday clothes.

"The fact that during his time there I never heard a bad word said about him from any of the coaching staff or the other players tells you a lot. That is quite unusual for a club.

"Celtic seem to have a very positive outlook on what the future will bring and that has a lot to do with having Henrik and Martin. It must be a dream for the manager to wake up every day knowing he has Henrik in the team and he must pray he stays fit and doesn't get hit with any more serious injuries.

"You only have to look at what happened during John Barnes' time at the club when Henrik broke his leg to understand how valuable he is.

"Rangers will feel they can hit back to become Scotland's top dogs again but I'm not so sure about that. I think if Henrik stays fit there is no reason why Celtic can't be champions for as long as he is in the team.

"He is contracted until the summer of 2004 and will honour that deal. I wouldn't bet against him leaving with three more league medals to add to the two he already has."

SILVER SERVICE: Henrik (far right) celebrates after a Cup final victory with Hogaborgs in 1980

PLAY TIME: Henrik (fourth from left) enjoys a laugh with his Hogaborgs team-mates

FEELING FRUITY: Larsson packed fruit and vegetables as a young man in Sweden while he tried to make the grade as a footballer – here he relaxes in his work overalls on a break with colleagues

SMILES BETTER: Henrik with pals at the Wieselgrensskolan recreation centre where he also worked before becoming a footballing superstar in Sweden and Scotland with Celtic

LAUGHING BHOY: a teenage Larsson clowns around with mates back home in Sweden

HIS GREATEST MATCH: Henrik is all smiles as he ties the knot with the beautiful Magdalena

PARADISE FOUND: a momentous day as Henrik joins Celtic on July 25, 1997 for £650,000

FALSE START: He's a hero now but Henrik's Celtic debut against Hibs turned into a nightmare as his misplaced pass set-up the Easter Road side's winner in a shock 2-1 defeat

HEAD BHOY: Larsson heads home his first league goal for the Hoops in a 2-0 win at St Johnstone

DREADLOCKED MASTER: Henrik's classy finishing started to make him a fans' favourite

MODEL PROFESSIONAL: No sign of the fruit packers overalls here as Henrik poses for a fashion shoot looking every bit the football superstar he has now become

CALL THE FASHION POLICE: Regi Blinker, Morten Wieghorst, Harald Brattbakk and Tom Boyd join Henrik for the Celtic players' Christmas lunch during season 97/98

COLD COMFORT: the weather might be bad but Henrik was beginning to enjoy life in Scotland

SMELLS LIKE TEAM SPIRIT: Under Wim Jansen, Celtic's players bonded magnificently

FIRM FAVOURITE: Henrik celebrates with Craig Burley after the midfielder's brilliant first goal in the 2-0 New Year win over Rangers in 1998 – the result proved critical in the championship chase

SAINT HENRIK: Larsson celebrates his great goal against St Johnstone in the title decider of 1998

BRATT'S IT: Harald's late strike v Saints sealed the title, much to the delight of Henrik and pals

THAT'S MY BHOY: Henrik and his son Jordan – named after Larsson's hero – Michael Jordan

FIRM FRIENDS: Giovanni van Bronckhorst remains great friends with his former Old Firm rival

FIRST CLASS COACH: Wim Jansen and Larsson celebrate the 1998 title triumph

TONGUE LASHING: Henrik plays to the fans after his last-gasp winner against Dundee in 1999

VID YOU BELIEVE IT: Larsson had struck up a fine partnership with Mark Viduka but tragedy struck in October 1999 when the Swedish hero broke his leg against Lyon in the UEFA Cup (below)

BACK IN THE GOAL ROUTINE: King Henrik showed he was back to his best after his horror injury with a super solo goal against Italy – who had the best defence in the tournament – at Euro 2000

S-MART MOVERS: The arrival of Martin O'Neill as Celtic boss in July 2000 signalled a rebirth for the Hoops and allowed Larsson to reach his full potential in a season of goals and glory

GOAL TWINS: Chris Sutton's signing heralded the beginning of a fabulous Celtic strike partnership

JOY OF SIX: Henrik goes wild after his stunning solo goal in the 6-2 victory over Rangers in August 2000

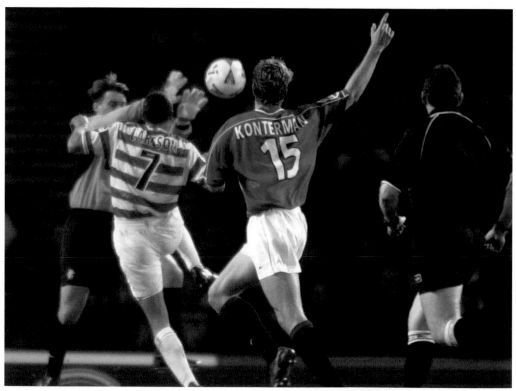

TASTY CHIP: Larsson lobs Klos to put Celtic on the road to CIS Cup semi-final victory against Rangers

HAT-TRICK HERO: Larsson completes his stunning treble in the 3-0 CIS Cup final win over Killie

A LEAGUE OF THEIR OWN: Tommy's goal against St Mirren secured the championship for Celts

BOOT-IFUL: Henrik's cup final double along with Jackie McNamara's strike won Celtic the treble

MAGIC MOMENT: Larsson laps up the crowd's adulation on the pitch after the 3-0 win over Hibs

GLORY BHOY: a sight to cheer the heart of every Celt – Henrik Larsson with trophy in hand

# six season 99-00

CELTIC'S 1999-2000 season ended at exactly 7.12pm on October 21 in Lyon's Stade de Gerland.

Before that UEFA Cup tie in France between Celtic and Lyon the Parkhead club were travelling through the season nicely, fighting it out with Rangers at the top of the SPL table and still in Europe and the League Cup.

But one sickening moment threw everything up in the air when Henrik Larsson sustained a double fracture of his left leg after a clash with French defender Serge Blanc. Celtic eventually lost 1-0, ironically with Blanc scoring the goal, but the result wasn't important at that time – the welfare of the fans' hero was.

The striker had to be pumped full of morphine to ease the pain for the flight home to Glasgow that Thursday night and rumours were rife that he would never kick a ball again. The nation appeared to be in a state of mourning.

Tributes from all over Europe poured into Celtic Park and the Larsson family home in Bothwell from Ally McCoist, Charlie Nicholas, Wim Jansen, the Feyenoord squad and Sweden manager Tommy Soderberg to name but a few.

Celtic were urged to go out and buy big to replace the superstar but didn't have the funds. Let's be honest, at that time you would have needed £10m to replace Henrik. Instead, Celtic signed veteran striker Ian Wright on a free transfer from West Ham. The former Arsenal and England star certainly had the pedigree and charisma to wipe away the tears that had flowed for Henrik in the dressing-room and in the stands. But he just didn't have the ability any more.

Celtic's season eventually crumbled. They crashed out of Europe to Lyon, were humiliated in the Scottish Cup 3-1 at home to Inverness Caledonian Thistle and lost the league title by 21 points to arch rivals Rangers. The only consolation was lifting the CIS League Cup after beating Aberdeen 2-0 at Hampden.

The biggest loser of all was head coach John Barnes. It was his first job in management and he needed all the help in the world. The former Liverpool and England winger appeared to have started well but Larsson's injury was as welcome to him as a hole in the head.

Cleverly, he tried to play it all down to keep the dressing-room in decent spirits and retain the belief that, despite Henrik's absence, Celtic could still win the league. Deep down, Barnes knew it was a battle he'd be unlikely to win as Larsson had been on fire up until that night, scoring a hat-trick against Aberdeen just four days before the injury to take his tally of Premier League goals to 50 in just over two seasons – the fastest half century recorded in the SPL.

The axe eventually fell on Barnes in February after the Caley Thistle defeat and he was shown the door along with assistant Eric Black. But there must be times when Barnes has looked at last season's Treble-winning side and wondered how things would have turned out if Henrik hadn't broken his leg.

Put it this way, would Martin O'Neill have three trophies in the bag if he had been minus the super striker for more than half a season?

Barnes can only think of what might have been and said: "We lost Henrik in October, and November was also a bad month for us – that was when I first felt it was starting to go wrong for me. It was no co-incidence we were without Henrik at the time. There is no doubt we would have had a far better chance of winning the league had he been fit. He was a huge, huge loss.

"But when we lost him I didn't want to just come right out and say it was a disaster, even though that was probably how I felt. We didn't have the quality within the squad to replace Larsson but I had to put on a brave face. I didn't want the players to become any more downbeat and make them feel we couldn't succeed without Henrik. I had to stay positive, no matter what I was feeling inside.

"It would have taken at least £10m to replace him and we just didn't have that sort of cash to spend on one player at that time. So the short-term solution was to bring in Wright. I have no regrets about that, although I could have spent two or three million on a striker had I wanted to. It just wasn't to be and I am sorry it didn't work out better. Celtic are a huge club."

Kenny Dalglish took over from Barnes but he also had to do without Larsson until the very last game of the season when the striker was fit enough to come on for the last 20 minutes in a victory over Dundee United.

But for almost three months prior to that Dalglish studied Larsson's every development, praying he would come back sooner rather than later to boost his team for the title run-in against Rangers. Henrik was eager to help out but was sensible enough not to risk his career by returning too soon for the sake of a dozen games.

Dalglish, who lost his job as Director of Football shortly after O'Neill was appointed as manager, recalled: "The last thing I wanted to do was rush Henrik back, even though I would love to have had him playing every week.

"I could see him getting better all the time and he was keen to be in the first team as quickly as possible. He made one or two comebacks in the reserves when maybe he wasn't quite right but told me before the Dundee United game he was ready for it and I was delighted to give him a taste of the action again.

"I knew I could trust his word because he is a man of integrity and a tremendous professional. I knew he wouldn't tell me a lie about his fitness and that's why I was happy to include him in the squad. He had so much to play for with Sweden in Euro 2000 and I knew he wouldn't jeopardise his career for the sake of one tournament.

93

"Everyone who knows Henrik and has ever worked with him will tell you he is an honest fella and when he looks you in the eye and tells you something you know it is the whole truth."

There has always been something special about Celtic's number seven jersey, graced in the past by such stars as Jimmy Johnstone, Dalglish himself and now Larsson. King Kenny was idolised in the 1970s before moving to Liverpool in 1977 for £440,000 but is still widely regarded as one of the – if not the – greatest player ever to have worn the Hoops.

Dalglish genuinely blushes when that is mentioned and, even if he did believe it, he knows he has severe competition in Larsson.

KD said: "I think Henrik is now as good as anyone in the game and the way he bounced back from injury to score 53 goals was unbelievable, a fairytale in fact. To score his 50th of the season at Ibrox must have been special, and the two in the Scottish Cup Final against Hibs was an ending to a season he probably thought he could only have dreamed about.

"Henrik has achieved enough with Celtic to stand beside any hero from the past. He is now an icon to millions of fans around the world, and rightly so.

"His attitude and mental strength are exceptional and he has the wonderful ability not to let missing a chance get him down. Simply, he has no fear. He keeps his head and bounces straight back to put the next chance in the net. That's a quality only top, top strikers have, and Henrik certainly falls into that category. He is a very single-minded character, too, like every great player must be. Yet he is so orientated towards the Celtic team, everyone who has played with him will tell you that."

The loss of Larsson left Australian striker Mark Viduka as the main goal threat, with the only back-up provided by Wright and young Mark Burchill.

Viduka, a snip at £3.5m from Croatia Zagreb a year earlier, rose above the adversity to score 27 goals that season and claim the prestigious PFA Players' Player of the Year award.

It wasn't enough to bring major honours but the giant striker could give no more in what turned out to be his last season in the hoops before joining David O'Leary's Leeds United for £6m.

Just after Larsson's tragic injury Viduka was on record as

saying: "Henrik will be badly missed because he is our main player. But I will miss him off the field just as much, as he is a good friend and you don't like to see things like that happen to people you care about. I am genuinely heartbroken for him.

"I want to make sure the team is winning to make the viewing from the stand for Henrik as enjoyable as possible. We don't want to be losing or not scoring goals so Henrik might feel he has to rush back to help us when he is not really ready.

"We have to win trophies but right now it feels like we have to do it even more so for Henrik's sake.

"I accept there will be higher expectations of me now that we will no longer have him for the rest of the season. I don't, however, have a problem with that.

"We also have Mark Burchill in the squad but I am that bit older and more experienced and playing a leading-the-line role is something I'm familiar with. I did it a lot at Croatia Zagreb and it's something I thrived on. Losing Henrik is a devastating blow to Celtic and it would be nice to put Lyon out for him, especially after the injury he suffered. And if we can do that then we have to think we can go on and win the league."

We all know how misguided that statement turned out to be.

Just days after the operation to mend his broken leg, Larsson spoke of the fears that his career could have been finished. He said: "All I remember about the incident was chasing their left wing-back and then he caught me on the back of the calf as we tackled and I went down. I heard something snap. When I rolled over and saw my leg I knew it was broken.

"Yes, I thought it might have ended my career. You do think of these things when you get a bad injury.

"Now, under the circumstances, I have to say I feel good. I have a lot to look forward to and plenty of time to recover. The doctors have not yet given me any indications of when I will be able to return. But I have to be patient and realistic. Next season has to be my aim but I will continue to think positively. I have my family and friends around me and that means so much. I have also received plenty of cards and flowers from people and I would like to thank them, it means so much to me."

Top orthopaedic surgeon Billy Leach was one of the horrified spectators in the Stade de Gerland that night.

Like the 37,500 fans at the game and the many more who watched on television in pubs and homes across Scotland, Leach was stunned by what he saw although he admits now it appeared much worse at the time than it actually was.

He said: "When you look at the photographs in the following day's newspapers it looks absolutely horrific because everyone thinks the bone had come through his sock.

"In fact, that was his shinpad. If the leg had broken the skin Henrik would have had to go to hospital in Lyon. While I'm sure the doctors there would have looked after him perfectly well we were glad to get him back to Glasgow."

As was wife Magdalena, one of the worried viewers as BBC Scotland replayed the incident over and over again. Five minutes after her husband collapsed in agony she received a call from a Celtic official confirming he had broken his leg.

Magdalena said: "Henrik came on the phone. He didn't say much – he had been given something for the pain and was screaming. He told me not to worry. They won't know how bad he is until they do X-rays but it looked horrible on TV. I am still in shock."

Understandably, the atmosphere on the flight home was suitably funereal with even the re-runs of comedy show *Frasier* unable to offer any respite from the gloom as Henrik lay across a row of seats in order to rest his broken tibia and fibula.

Everyone present had already realised that the striker's – and, by extension, Celtic's – season was over. The worry then was if he would ever be the same again.

Fortunately, he wouldn't. He became even better, although luck played its part in that.

Leach added: "There were no complications. The skin hadn't been broken so there was no open wound, which meant no possibility of contamination at the time of the injury.

"It was as straightforward as these things go while still being severe enough.

"I didn't see Henrik professionally until the following afternoon. The first thing I told him was he would be out for 10 months and should forget about playing for Sweden at Euro 2000.

"At the back of my mind I thought he might have an outside

chance of making that tournament but it would have been wrong of me to say so because it remained highly unlikely.

"A recent study conducted in the USA specifically on soccer players revealed the average recovery time for such an injury is 10 months. That's why I said he should bank on NOT being at Euro 2000 and that anything else would be a wonderful bonus.

"Obviously, everyone is different but Henrik's recovery was nothing short of phenomenal. Club physio Brian Scott also played a huge part.

"There are certain things we know which impede the healing process. Smoking is one, and if you're a big boozer that won't help either. Taking anti-inflammatory pills is another no-no.

"None of those things applied to Henrik, who did everything he was told and more. I have to say his desire to rehabilitate was nothing short of tremendous.

"I've discovered over the years that a lot boils down to the attitude and determination of the individual patient to recover.

"In surgery, when you start off you tend to think it's all about how well you do. But it's the people who want to get better who get better quickest. Having the right frame of mind is a huge prognostic indicator."

First on the scene that fateful night when Henrik collapsed on the turf was Vidar Riseth. He dashed over to see his close friend and team-mate and knew immediately things were serious.

Indeed, the injury looked so severe that the versatile Norwegian, signed by Dr Venglos the previous season for £1.2m, had to turn away when he came close to being sick.

Riseth said: "I was only about 20 metres away from Henrik when he fell and I ran over to him as fast as I could.

"When I got there I could see he was in distress and then I caught a look at his leg dangling in the air. I felt really sick and had to turn away.

"It was the worst injury I'd ever seen and I hope never to see anything even close to it again. Yet it was a complete accident and nobody at Celtic held the Lyon player responsible. It all happened because Henrik tracked back to help out the team, typical of his great attitude.

"It was a painful sight and I felt so ill because Henrik is a very good friend and I don't like to see people in such agony. I felt so sorry for him, to watch him lying there helpless. It was so unusual to see him unable to help himself.

"It really put the whole team off and, as everyone knows, we lost that match 1-0 and crashed out of the competition a couple of weeks later. But the damage was a lot worse than just losing the European tie.

"I think the Henrik thing shattered everybody and we never recovered. It was hard enough trying to catch Rangers without having to do it without our match winner. Our fans felt it, too. It was just too much for the club.

"Henrik went to hospital after the game and had to take painkillers and injections to make the flight home as comfortable as possible. I spoke to him on the plane as he was sprawled out across three seats with his leg in plaster and he was obviously sore and upset. It is difficult to know what to say because no amount of words can compensate for what happened. But you have to at least try.

"But the operation went very well in Glasgow and he was back in at Parkhead not long after. But I remember him arriving for the first time since the break and he walked in on crutches. He couldn't function without them.

"I thought to myself 'Oh my God, he's not going to make it' but I should have known better. I walked straight up to him and said 'Henrik, you are going to be okay' and he said 'Yes, Vidar. Don't worry, I will be back better than ever'. And I could see in his eyes that he meant it.

"It wasn't long before the crutches were dumped and he was on his way back to normal. He seemed so determined to return and prove a lot of doubters wrong.

"It had been suggested by many people on different occasions that his career was over, or if he did come back he would be nowhere near as good.

"The fightback was on and he was in the gym first thing in the morning, before anyone else arrived, for training with Brian Scott and was one of the last to leave. Henrik really worked his backside off. In fact, he was probably grafting harder than a lot of the guys who were fit."

It came as no surprise to Riseth when Larsson made it back to the first team on the last day of the season in a victory against

Dundee United when he came off the bench to a standing ovation and ran on to the park to the theme tune from *The Magnificent Seven.*

There was a lump in Riseth's throat and he said: "It was a great day and at least every Celtic fan finished the season with a smile on the face, although we would love to have won the league.

"But Henrik was pleased to be back and was a happy man to get through that game unscathed. It was the first step after a long recovery and he deserved it."

Lyon defender Blanc was another person delighted to see Henrik bounce back in such fine style – in fact, it would have been difficult to find a more relieved man on the planet.

The Frenchman has been unable to speak to Larsson personally, as Lyon's strict rules prevent communicating one-to-one with opponents, even under those circumstances. But he did send a get-well card and gifts to show he cared about Henrik and wanted him back playing as quickly as possible.

Blanc said: "I am very happy he has made such a perfect return to football and I was delighted to hear he had a such a good season on a personal level and a good season for his club, too.

"I hope this doesn't sound callous, but I did not blame myself for the injury. I just happened to be the player involved when Henrik went down but I do not accept responsibility for his broken leg. I'm sure he will understand what I mean.

"I have seen a similar injury and that is why when I looked down at the time I had to turn away. It really did break my heart and I was shocked by it all.

"It was a very unfortunate incident and I wish it had never happened. But it was about two committed footballers playing at the highest level in a very big match and sometimes these kind of things happen. That's a shame, but he has bounced back magnificently

"I was very upset at the time because Henrik looked in a lot of pain and I am so happy to know he has fully recovered and is probably a better player now than he has ever been. I wish him all the best for the rest of his career with Celtic and Sweden."

# seven season 00-01

BROKEN LEG? What broken leg? For Henrik Larsson, his team-mates and adoring legions of fans it was as though Lyon had never happened.

And if season 1999/2000 had been the striker's annus horribilus then 2000/01 was his annus mirabilis. He grabbed 53 goals in 53 appearances to set a post-war record and won UEFA's Golden Shoe as the top scorer in European league football, pipping the likes of Parma's Enrico Chiesa, Roma's Gabriel Batistuta and AC Milan's Andrei Shevchenko.

Larsson's goals propelled Celtic to the dizzy heights of their first Treble since 1969. The league was won at a canter with arch-rivals Rangers left demoralised by four severe beatings in the league and CIS Cup. And in two cup finals Henrik wrote himself into Hampden history with five incredible goals.

Such success – and the scenes of unrestrained euphoria that greeted them – must have seemed a million miles away when the Celtic squad turned up for their first day of pre-season training.

To add to the shambles of the previous term they had lost the powerful Australian striker Mark Viduka to Leeds. After a typically tortuous summer of speculation, Martin O'Neill had been brought in as manager.

The Derry man was a great player with Nottingham Forest and Northern Ireland, winning a European Cup winner's medal and appearing in the World Cup Finals. He had achieved relative success as manager at Leicester City. But the task facing him at Parkhead that summer was enormous. He promised he would do everything he could to bring success to the club. And he did.

Rangers, O'Neill said, were the benchmark. But he had no doubt who the linchpin of his side would be. Martin said he had always known Larsson was a good player. But not until he'd seen him for himself did he realise he was wrong – for the Swede was a GREAT player. The shrewd boss immediately supplied his talisman with an accomplice. At a cost of £6m, the rugged Chris Sutton was rescued from a miserable spell at Chelsea.

Another key signing was the pacy Belgian defender Joos Valgaeren, who had impressed O'Neill with his displays at Euro 2000. The fans also "discovered" a superbly-skilled left winger – Dutchman Bobby Petta, who had struggled so badly under the Barnes-Dalglish regime.

Most of all Celtic rediscovered their pride. Under this manager they would fight for the jersey to the finish. He gave players back their confidence. And despite what he was telling the press, Martin demanded his players believe they would win the league.

The story of the season was encapsulated in the first 90 minutes of the league campaign at Tannadice. Henrik scored with a fantastic left-foot curler before Dundee United equalised. But as the final whistle neared, Celtic refused to take anything less than three points. From a Stephane Mahe shot a scramble resulted in Sutton poking home the winner. O'Neill's men were on their way.

Anyone who doubted that was about to be given a rude awakening. In one of the most sensational matches ever seen at Celtic Park, Rangers were demolished 6-2 with Henrik scoring two beauties after the Ibrox men had threatened to fight back from an early goal blitz by Sutton, Stilian Petrov and Paul Lambert.

The scoring was finished off in style in the last minute when Mahe rampaged down the left and crossed for Sutton to steer home the sixth. That rout gave the Celtic players and their fans the confidence to believe they were in at the start of something extra special, which pleased no one more than the ever-enthusiastic French defender Mahe.

Stephane – who moved on from Parkhead in August to join Craig Levein's Hearts at Tynecastle – is a huge admirer of Henrik the footballer. But he is even more a fan of Henrik the person.

Now Mahe has a had a chance to step back from the Parkhead scene he has evaluated what it meant to play for Celtic... and what it was like to see Larsson close up away from park, handling the publicity and being constantly in demand as he enjoyed the year of his life in football with the prestigious Golden Shoe waiting at the end.

Mahe is honoured to have been there for it all and said: "I was signed by Wim Jansen and spent four great years with Celtic, winning many trophies.

"Yes, Henrik was very special to the team and we couldn't have done it without him. That is obvious after the 53 goals he scored last season, an amazing record.

"But for me, Henrik Larsson the man is the best of all. He has a lovely personality and is a beautiful person who always has time for people and nice words to say about people.

"Sometimes dressing-rooms can be strange places and not everyone gets on with everyone all the time. It happens in every job in the world and is a fact of life.

"But I never, ever heard Henrik say a bad word about anyone and I never heard him talk behind someone's back.

"That is a special quality in my eyes, the thing that makes him a special man.

"I remember when I was sent off by Hugh Dallas against Rangers in 1999 and they clinched the league back from Celtic that day. I sat in the dressing-room very upset and wondering what my team-mates would say to me. I thought they might blame me and accuse me of letting them down.

"Henrik came in and had some great words of comfort. He was honest and sincere and told me to get it out of my head right away. He said something along the lines of it wasn't like I had killed someone, it was only a game of football and I had to forget about it and get on with my career at Celtic. The other players were supportive, too, and I appreciated that."

Stephane also has great memories from last season but is just disappointed he wasn't on the field more often to lap them up.

He said: "I had a lot of injuries, and when I was fit it was impossible to get back into the team because everyone was in exceptional form.

"I would love to have been out there helping the boys to win every game but I had to settle for a place in the stand watching Henrik and the rest of the guys performing so well.

"For Henrik to achieve so much last season after his injury was truly incredible, and he has himself and the Celtic medical team to thank. I also think Stilian will come back stronger and better than ever from his injury. I wish him all the best. But back to Henrik. Martin was the perfect manager for him to have at that time as he demanded 100 per cent from every player in every minute of every game.

"If you didn't give that, the boss soon let you know. I'm not saying Henrik wouldn't have given his all but it was important for him to have a boss capable of getting the best out of everyone.

"It led to us winning every trophy and it was a very happy place to be at. It was special for Henrik, Paul Lambert, Jonathan Gould and myself because we were the survivors bought by Wim who won the title three years earlier. Tom Boyd, Jackie McNamara, Alan Stubbs and Tommy Johnson were also there at that time.

"I will never forget my time at Celtic. Last season, the 6-2 win over Rangers sticks out. I really enjoyed that game and we scored many good goals, including Henrik's little chip over the keeper in the second half."

Yet when Mahe arrived from Rennes in a £500,000 deal in the summer of 1997, as one of Jansen's first signings, he walked into the dressing-room totally ignorant of his team-mates.

He said: "I didn't know who Henrik was and didn't know anything about him. Maybe if you read the papers every day or watch worldwide football on television you will know everything but I don't do that. It is a big, big world out there and it is impossible to know every player from every country. But I soon learned about Henrik and could see within a short space of time that he was special. He has great close control, good pace and is a great finisher.

"One of his greatest qualities is his strength, He protects the ball well from defenders and it is impossible to knock him off it. I found that in training every day and it was hard to resist not having a go at him in other ways to get possession.

"It is the same for every defender and he is just about impossible to stop. Now I am playing for Hearts I appreciate how difficult it is for other clubs to face Celtic when Henrik is in the team.

"Even if you put four or five men on him it doesn't guarantee anything. I can tell you defenders sit in the dressing-room not looking forward to playing against Henrik. You just have to hope he has an off-day... and that never happens.

"He also loves scoring goals. He has a look of real joy when he sees the ball in the net because it gives him pleasure and it pleases thousands of other people. With Henrik in the team it really is hard to see Celtic not doing well. They are now the club everyone has to try and keep up with and it will not be easy because they play with such confidence and have a very happy dressing-room.

"I wish them all the best but I now want to do well with Hearts. Craig has signed me and I owe him a lot. I want to repay him by helping my new team into back into European football next season."

So far, Larsson has carried on from where he left off in the last campaign and his goals and assists have already won crucial games. And Mahe is of the opinion that the super Swede's game is going to get better and better.

Stephane said: "I don't know if Henrik will ever score 53 goals again in one season but he will come close, that is for sure.

"Perhaps though – and just as importantly – I think he will improve as a player. He is not the type of person to sit back and believe he has done it all. He has an incredible appetite for the game and always believes he is capable of better.

"He does extra training and works tirelessly on his shooting and close-range finishing. That kind of attitude only leads to one thing and that is up the way, not down or staying at the same level.

"I have been lucky to play with some great players during my career in France with Paris St Germain and Auxerre, men like Youri Djorkaeff, Enzo Schifo and Stephane Guivarc'h. I faced Chris Waddle many times and he was a very difficult opponent. I would have to put Henrik on the same level, at the very least, as all of them. Yes, he is one of the best I have ever played with.

"And when my children and grand-children ask me about my career, Henrik's name will always be in the conversation. That is one of the best compliments I can pay him."

As the season went on Celtic's confidence grew as O'Neill brought in more shrewd signings. Didier Agathe, from the tiny island of Reunion, had his short-term contract at Hibs bought out for a measly £50,000. He was soon terrorising left-backs with his blistering pace down the right wing.

Alan Thompson from Aston Villa supplied craft and graft on the left side of midfield while Rab Douglas came from Dundee and went on to replace Gould in goal.

In the wake of the season's worst result, a 5-1 defeat at Ibrox, Martin moved swiftly to sign Ramon Vega on loan after the towering Swiss defender had endured an unhappy spell in the Spurs reserves. He also stepped up his bid to land the battling Northern Ireland midfielder Neil Lennon from Leicester.

As a welcome Christmas present to his fans, Henrik scored a great hat-trick at home to Aberdeen. The game marked Vega's Celtic debut and he capped it with two goals. He had much more to celebrate before the end of the season and had no doubt about who was most responsible for his sizeable collection of winner's medals and bonuses.

Vega is certainly the first to admit he would rather play with Henrik than against him. Having had the awesome task of trying to mark the Swede in the past he is well aware of the qualities that make him so deadly.

Since they first clashed as teenagers, Ramon has developed a heartfelt admiration for Larsson's qualities and has charted his progress with interest. His respect and appreciation for the striker's deadly blend of silk and steel only deepened during the five months they spent as team-mates at Parkhead.

Larsson was one of the few players Vega was aware of when O'Neill rescued him from his Tottenham misery in December, but he was astounded to discover from working with Henrik every day at training that he was an even better player than he originally thought.

Ramon, who has since signed for Gianluca Vialli's Watford on a Bosman during the close season, said: "Henrik is a very good finisher but he's also an unselfish team player. You usually find, even with international strikers, they are either one thing or the other but Henrik has both. That is his main quality.

"You can see by his record that he specialises in big games. He showed that quite often in the time I was at Celtic. He was on fire in most matches anyway but he was a major, major player in the Old Firm clashes and big cup ties.

"People are happy to play alongside him. He's a very important figure at the club because his goals can take the pressure off everyone else. The qualities he has are very difficult to find, especially in a striker, which is why everyone worries when he picks up the slightest knock."

Ramon had enjoyed success in his homeland with Grasshoppers of Zurich but that was nothing compared to the intensity of his experience with Celtic. The size of the crowds and the outpouring of emotion that followed as first the CIS Cup, then the league championship, and finally, the Tennent's Scottish Cup were secured will live with him forever.

Vega reflected: "My whole time at Parkhead was special. To win all three trophies was tremendous but my favourite memories of Henrik – and there are many – concern the two cup finals which he really won for us by himself. He scored every goal in the CIS Final when we beat Kilmarnock 3-0 and, when we went back to Hampden for the last time, he scored two of our three goals when we won against Hibs.

"I think that last match stands out particularly because both finishes were absolutely magnificent.

"But throughout my time there, even when the games weren't too good and we were having a hard time, even when Henrik wasn't having one of his best days, there was always the possibility he would conjure a goal out of nothing.

"We always hoped he would have at least one chance to score

because he was often our only hope! It says a lot about his quality that he almost always managed to get that goal.

"For me, it was a fantastic experience to play alongside Henrik in that special team."

Like everyone else in and out of football Vega has nothing but positive things to say about the Swede. Which only confirms that you don't need to behave like George Best or Diego Maradona to play like them.

The big man said: "Henrik is a very quiet person but likes to look after his team-mates. He's very grounded and a great professional. I admire him as much off the pitch as I do on it."

The two men again found themselves on opposing sides towards the end of last season when their countries met in a friendly in Switzerland. Just for a change, Henrik didn't score but helped team-mate Anders Svensson to a double in Sweden's 2-0 win.

Ramon admitted: "It's always very difficult to play against a striker who is in hot form and when our countries met Henrik was at the top of his game, absolutely.

"He had been scoring regularly for a year since coming back from his injury. He had 50-odd goals under his belt and was full of confidence.

"However, because he was my team-mate at that time we had an understanding – we didn't want to damage each other.

"That match against Sweden was two weeks before the Scottish Cup final and I remember saying: 'Listen, Henrik, let's reserve something for THAT game, okay?' But even in a friendly he was a tough opponent. I would much rather have him in my team than play against him any time."

Vega revealed that Larsson's talent and will to win are not just confined to the football pitch – he's also a fierce competitor on the fairways and greens. The stopper said: "I played golf against him and he's extremely good at that, too, after being in Scotland for so long. He came to the best country in the world to learn that particular sport and he's picked it up quickly.

"He's actually a remarkable golfer – it could well be his next profession after he stops playing football, so I'm still trying to find something he isn't good at!"

It's been a long search and one that shows no sign of ending in the near future. Ramon recalled: "I knew about Henrik long before I joined Celtic. In fact, I first came across him 10 years ago when I was playing for Grasshoppers and we faced each other for our national Under-21 teams in Sweden.

"At that time Grasshoppers wanted to buy him but the move didn't happen and he ended up going to Feyenoord.

"Henrik was top quality even at that age and I took an interest in his career and I've followed it with interest ever since.

"Last season was the only time I had the chance to watch him up close and it turned out to be the best one he's ever had – so far! I hope he can do at least as well again because that would be fantastic for him and for Celtic.

"Larsson's definitely among the top 10 strikers I've ever played with or against, including Ronaldo, Shearer, Henry, Owen and Zola. It's difficult to put them in order because every one is a different type – one may be a lethal finisher, another may be more skilful, another may be good in the air, and so on.

"I loved operating behind Henrik and Chris Sutton because it meant I always had the right options when it came to playing the ball out of defence.

"They were both good in the air and could hold the ball up, plus Henrik is also very fast. So I could play the ball short or long and they would usually make something of it.

"Henrik also comes deep looking for the ball and that makes it difficult for defenders to mark him. He makes great runs into channels and that combination helps explain why he is such an extraordinary striker."

It's hardly surprising, then, to hear that Vega believes the club's superb achievements last season would have been practically impossible without Henrik's prolific scoring.

He said: "To be honest, we probably had a 40 per cent or more chance of winning games with him in the team, because he was the one getting most of the goals and often he really won the matches for us. I can't say we wouldn't have won the league or one of the cups if he hadn't been there, although it's a possibility we wouldn't have been successful in all three. Let's just say it would have been much more difficult without him."

Which is saying plenty. It was a case of cometh the hour cometh the man. When the big occasion demanded it, Henrik delivered in spades.Four Hampden appearances produced nine goals. He also bagged six against Rangers to demoralise Celtic's main rivals for the title.

The destination of the first trophy of the season, the CIS Insurance Cup, was decided on March 18 when Kilmarnock were routed 3-0 at the national stadium thanks to an outstanding hat-trick from the goal machine.

It was a win made all the more impressive by the fact that Celtic – for whom the relatively inexperienced trio of Stephen Crainey, Jamie Smith and Colin Healy all made contributions – were forced to play for the last 30 minutes without Sutton.

The big hitman was shown the red card by referee Hugh Dallas for a foul on Gary Holt. The pre-match favourites were only 1-0 ahead at the time but held on resolutely then destroyed Killie on the break.

Sutton had already played his part in the opener shortly after the interval, nodding on a Vega header for Henrik to score with an acrobatic scissors kick.

Larsson's second, 16 minutes from time after a sublime pass from Lubomir Moravcik, was a shot from the edge of the box that deflected off Chris Innes on its way into the net.

But the third was the pick of the bunch. The rampant Swede beat Kevin McGowne just inside the Celtic half and raced clear of the chasing pack before bamboozling Gordon Marshall with an audacious drag-back and then, and only then, sticking the ball into a  gaping net.

Afterwards Henrik grinned: "It's always satisfying when you win, especially in a cup final. I'd had the good luck to lift this trophy in my first season but I didn't play in the final last year.

"I could never have imagined then, or any other time, that I would score 47 goals. You can't even dream about that, it's tremendous. Then again, if the team is playing well and providing the strikers with the right service that makes it easier."

Larsson also highlighted the mental toughness of O'Neill's men after Sutton's dismissal.

He said: "That just shows you the kind of character this team has. Being 1-0 ahead at the time made things a lot easier but no one was prepared to give up and that's why we finished winning by three.

"It was hard to make the breakthrough, though. If there were any chances in that first half I don't remember them."

Henrik also paid tribute to the contribution O'Neill and his backroom staff John Robertson and Steve Walford made in transforming the shell of a squad left behind by their predecessors.

The hitman said: "The boss's influence shows on the whole team. He brought back a lot of self-confidence to the players who were here and also to the ones he brought in. You could see that in the performances of the younger guys. They haven't played so much this season but did extremely well. They want to show they should be in the first team every week."

The championship race, which had seemed a foregone conclusion for months, was finally clinched on April 7 with five games to spare as St Mirren were beaten 1-0 in front of an ecstatic Parkhead crowd. Astonishingly, Henrik didn't score although he might have grabbed the glory for himself.

Instead, typically, he unselfishly rolled the ball to Tommy Johnson in a better position and, at the second attempt, the Englishman slotted it home.

As usual, Henrik was quick to pay tribute to the efforts of others. He said: "I've had players like Chris Sutton helping up front and it can't be forgotten how important he has been in this title run. Simon Donnelly and I did well together when we won it last time but this has been different. Chris takes the physical pressure off me.

"Didier Agathe and Bobby Petta have also played crucial parts because they give us width. You need that in today's game, especially playing for a club like Celtic because other teams come to Parkhead to defend and we need wide men who can get behind them."

The Swede preferred not to make comparisons between O'Neill and Jansen, who guided Celtic to a double in 1998. In fact, he couldn't have sidestepped the issue with greater ease if it had been Bert Konterman in front of him.

Larsson insisted: "Martin has been terrific but both men have great qualities. Wim won the league on a small budget but it was important he did that because it stopped Rangers making it 10 in a row. It feels great to have clinched the title again but you can't compare this with 1998. I'm just pleased the supporters got the party they wanted.

"It wasn't as tense as last time because we knew we'd have another chance if we didn't beat St Mirren. But we won in the end and now must wait and see what more we can achieve."

Henrik timed the astounding conclusion to his incredible scoring run to perfection. He notched number 50 at Ibrox, the final twist of the knife to add to their Old Firm rivals' agony. Moravcik also scored two great goals in a 3-0 thrashing.

Number 51 came in a 5-2 win over third-placed Hibs at Easter Road, though the match will be remembered more for the scoring return of Alan Stubbs after his second recovery from cancer.

The league season finally over, all eyes turned to Hampden Park on a gloriously sunny May afternoon as Celtic attempted to complete their first Treble since Jock Stein's all-conquering side 32 years earlier.

Hibs were the opposition but yet again had no answer to the Larsson Factor. To the delight of bookies everywhere, he failed to score the opening goal. Instead, Jackie McNamara – an early sub for the injured Moravcik – provided a cute finish from Agathe's clever through ball.

However, normal service was resumed three minutes after the break when Henrik supplied an unsaveable finish to McNamara's cutback. And he completed the scoring when converting the penalty he won himself after outmuscling Hibs' centre-back Gary Smith.

Larsson said: "It has been an absolutely amazing season, and this just caps it all. A lot of people have spoken about my scoring run but you have to remember this is a team game and everyone from the management down has played their part in a tremendous achievement.

"It has been an incredible turnaround in our fortunes and we have managed to be consistent all season. There has been a lot of talk about the Treble but now that we have finally won it, it's something we will talk about with great pride."

It was a season when Henrik could do little wrong. He accounted for 53 of Celtic's 134 goals and in spite of coming in for some heavy treatment from defenders everywhere was cautioned only twice, which speaks volumes for his restraint.

Restraint, however, is not a word often associated with former Parkhead star Paolo di Canio. The gifted Italian also graced the No.7 jersey and he, too, was adored by the fans. But that's where the similarities between him and Larsson end.

Di Canio was a legend for a year in Glasgow after Tommy Burns paid AC Milan £1m for him in the summer of 1996. Paolo was an unbelievable entertainer... with a temper to match.

It was thought the man with golden boots would stop Rangers clinching nine-in-a-row. But he couldn't and parted company with the Hoops a few weeks later after a public and bitter dispute with Fergus McCann.

The Italian claimed he had a gentleman's agreement with the club's supremo that if he performed well his annual salary would be upped to a more appropriate level. McCann, of course, denied this and the wrangling is still going on.

The truth is out there somewhere, though, and will probably be revealed in court.

Di Canio was eventually sold – sorry, traded – to Sheffield Wednesday just days after Jansen took over in a deal worth £3m to Celtic, with Regi Blinker thrown in. The fans mourned the loss of their hero.

But little did they know the man with the dreadlocks and the white headband was about to step in and erase the memory of Paolo forever.

Larsson arrived just as di Canio was packing his belongings and they never got the chance to play in the same side together. But di Canio didn't need a close-up of Henrik to conclude that the hitman is right out of the top drawer.

He has watched Larsson many times on television and played against him in a pre-season friendly for West Ham during O'Neill's early days in charge.

Di Canio is a self-confessed fan of the super Swede and is delighted to see the club has managed to keep its most prized possession for the rest of his career at the top level.

The mercurial magician said: "Henrik is a very lucky man to be playing for Celtic and the fans are lucky to have such a good player doing so well every week.

"I know how it feels to be idolised by the Celtic fans – it is special. There isn't a better feeling in football than to hear them chant your name when you score a goal or produce a piece of skill. When the stands are packed with 60,000 supporters they make an incredible noise. Sometimes it was impossible to hear what your team-mates were saying out on the pitch.

"Henrik has them all shouting for him all the time and that must make him and his family feel very proud.

"I am pleased for the supporters that he is staying for the next three or four years. They deserve to have him because they put their heart and soul, not to mention their money, into the club and that should give them a right to see the very best.

"There are times I wish I was still with Celtic, feeling what Henrik feels all the time. But it wasn't the fans I had a fall-out with, it was Fergus McCann and we cannot turn the clock back. I had to do what I felt was the correct thing to do.

"I have had some good years in England but I do wish I was with Celtic to win the League. I was very pleased for them to clinch the Treble last season and to do it in such style against Rangers was so pleasant. I was also happy for Henrik to score all those goals and win the Golden Shoe award. It is not easy to turn on the style every week of the season, no matter the league you are playing in.

"He deserves everything because he is, without doubt, one of the best finishers in European football. If he decided to try and play in another league he could do it without any problem for any team he wanted to.

"But Henrik will be sticking with Celtic and the fans deserve to applaud themselves for that, because I'm sure the way they treat him was one of the main reasons he stayed.

"Now I hope he and Celtic can have another memorable year. I don't see any reason why they can't, because the club is in good hands with ambitious people who want to take it forward as far as possible."

The adulation for Larsson is not confined to one half of the Old Firm. He has enough talent for even the most faithful of Rangers followers to appreciate him The Ibrox players who come up against Henrik regularly are only too ready to acknowledge he has an abundance of talent. And who could blame the Light Blues for occasionally wishing he would leave Celtic to give them a better chance of winning back the SPL title?

In recent interviews about Larsson, Ibrox skipper Barry Ferguson – who voted for Larsson as his PFA Player of the Year for last season – said: "It is not good news for us that Henrik has signed a new deal with Celtic. If I'm being totally honest, I'd rather he hadn't stayed.

"He is a big threat to us – a genuine world-class player because you can't give him a sniff of the ball or it will end up in the net.

"Henrik pops up and scores even when he's not been having the greatest of games, and that is the difference between a good striker and a class one.

"Defenders always have to be extra careful with Larsson around. He must be a nightmare to try and mark as he never stands still, whether his team or the opposition has the ball. But he doesn't run about for the sake of it. His movement is clever.

"Everyone with leanings towards Celtic will be delighted to know he's pledged his future to the club. Deep down I have tremendous respect for him for the way he conducts himself and for the way he has bounced back from a serious injury to score 53 goals last season and help Celtic lift every prize in Scotland.

"Larsson is a great footballer and, apart from his skill and ability to score goals, he can also take a hard kick here and there without moaning or feigning injury. Mind you, he can also give it out when he wants. He is not shy in any way when it comes to that. Not that I'm moaning, it is part and parcel of football.

"I suppose another way of looking at it is that it means if we do win the league in the coming season nobody will be able to say we only managed it because Larsson wasn't there.

"We'll just need to wait and see what happens. I just hope there isn't a repeat of last season. But we will do our best to come back because nobody at Rangers wants to miss out two years in a row.

"We didn't enjoy seeing Celtic winning everything and it will be very interesting to see how it all unfolds."

The best season of Larsson's life ended with him picking up both the SPFA Player of the Year and the Football Writers' Player of the Year awards.

His incredible goal-scoring run led to some serious attention from other European giants. At various times Manchester

United and Barcelona were credited with being interested enough to consider offers around £15m.

Larsson still had two years of his contract to run but O'Neill felt the time was right to send out a loud and clear message by starting negotiations to make him the highest paid player at the club on a salary of around £40,000 per week until the summer of 2004.

The talks seemed to last forever. For six months hardly a day passed that the back pages weren't full of information or speculation on the biggest story of the season.

The long-running saga was settled during the summer of 2001 when Larsson put pen to paper in Sweden after Celtic chairman Brian Quinn flew there to hammer out the finer points with agent Rob Jansen.

A sigh of relief reverberated around every Celtic-supporting home in Scotland and beyond – with the biggest of all in the office of Martin O'Neill. The rest of the squad were also well chuffed and even those who had left, such as Vidar Riseth, still kept in constant touch with developments.

The big Norwegian was delighted to hear it had all been sorted because he felt that if Larsson had been allowed to leave it would have been the DEATH of the club he and millions of others care so deeply about.

Speaking from Germany, where he now stars for 1860 Munich, Vidar said: "I always thought Celtic would agree with Henrik on a new contract because it didn't make sense to do anything else.

"No matter the fee they might have received, it wouldn't have been nearly enough. He is priceless and I don't think any other striker would have scored the amount of goals he did last season, not to mention the ones he set up for others.

"Maybe Celtic didn't receive any official offers but they must have had inquiries and his agent must have been asked about Henrik's availability on many occasions from different top clubs around Europe.

"If Celtic had sold Henrik the share price would have fallen and the fans would have demonstrated because I think he must be the best player ever to turn out for the club. That would more or less have been the end of Celtic.

"But it all got sorted out and it is great for Celtic and for Henrik because he loves Scotland and so does his family.

"I know that for a fact, as all the Scandinavian players at the club were very close. We even allowed Regi Blinker to join in with us. We used to pretend he was half-Scandinavian to make him feel a proper part of it all. We would all meet regularly and have Christmas dinner together, having fun, cracking jokes and singing Christmas songs in our languages. Yes, Henrik even got involved in the singing but he doesn't have the best of voices!

"Mind you, he's good at just about everything else and is such a nice man. Even though I miss being at Celtic and miss Glasgow, I don't miss having to try and mark Henrik at training. It was a nightmare. He was so quick and never stood still, always on the move. In fact, he is the best I have ever played with – and I have played with brilliant guys such as Ole Gunnar Solksjaer and Tore Andre Flo.

"I used to come off the training pitch shattered mentally and physically after a session against him. It was the same with Mark Viduka. Both are highly talented players.

"Henrik also used to make a point of coming up to me after training, put his arm around me and tell me I played well if he thought I had done so.

"I think he liked to let us know he appreciated our efforts and watched us closely, rather than just getting plaudits all to himself and not bothering about the rest of us. That tells you a lot about him. He doesn't act like a star.

"Whether you are a farmer or a famous actor he will always make time for you. Not every special footballer is like that."

O'Neill sold Riseth during last season to 1860 Munich for £1m. Vidar wasn't assured of a regular first-team game as the Irishman started to shape his own squad of title-winners.

The Norwegian was heartbroken to leave but felt back in the Celtic swing of things from the moment he arrived in his new dressing-room to meet his team-mates.

He said: "Thomas Hassler is a very friendly guy. He is a legend in Germany and one of the best players the country has ever produced but he is down to earth.

"Thomas also knows his football inside-out as he makes a point of keeping up to date with most of the leagues in Europe.

"As soon as I walked into the 1860 dressing-room he welcomed me and asked what it was like at Celtic as he knew everything about the Old Firm games and the special atmosphere. He knew all about Henrik too and asked me if he had achieved so much because he is so good or because the Scottish League is of poor quality.

"Of course, I said it is all down to Henrik, as the competition in Scotland is not easy and that is the truth. Also, Henrik has scored plenty of goals at international level and we all know you don't get an easy game on that stage.

"I think Thomas was kind of hoping I could have brought Henrik with me but we both knew that was impossible. However, this is a guy who has played in the World Cup Final and starred for Inter Milan and Roma. They don't speak about other players unless they rate them and admire them."

But the chat about Henrik didn't stop there. Riseth soon found out he had entered a Larsson-mania zone and had to answer questions from the players of the European Cup holders, Bayern Munich.

Vidar said: "When I got a house out here it was in the same area as some of the Bayern players, such as the Brazilian striker Giovanni Elber. He really is a nice guy and we have spent a lot of time in each other's company.

"He is always asking about Henrik. He seemed to know quite a bit about him and wanted me to tell him what it was like to train and play beside him.

"Gio really is keen on him and that is some compliment because he is a striker of the highest quality. All good hitmen compare themselves with the best and strive to reach the heights of the guys who do it week-in, week-out."

Larsson is in that bracket and Riseth believes the Swede will stay there because he is a perfectionist and slaughters himself if he hasn't scored a goal or has played below the level he is capable of.

Vidar has witnessed the usually mild-mannered Larsson in some foul moods. He said: "Henrik is not a selfish player and will always put the team first. If he has a chance to score but a team-mate is in a better position, he will pass 100 times out of 100.

"But he still loves scoring – all good strikers do. In many ways they live for football. Seeing the ball bulging in the back of the net is what it is all about for those guys.

"Henrik gets very angry with himself if he feels he hasn't played well or has maybe missed a chance, and it is easy to tell when he is not happy. He sits in the dressing-room at the interval and it looks as though he is running through things in his mind, determined not to make the same mistake in the next half. But normal service is resumed quickly and before we know it a bit of boom-boom is there and he has scored a couple of goals. Great."

Riseth also puts his pal's incredible form down to O'Neill and believes the Celtic boss deserves enormous credit.

He said: "I have a lot of respect for Martin. Many people think we had a big fall-out and that is why I left but that is not true. We got on well and wished each other all the best when I was transferred.

"Celtic are the biggest and best club I have ever played for and it comforts me to still feel part of that. I still go back when I can and still get a lot of mail from Celtic fans. I appreciate that they write to me even though I am in Germany.

"Martin is a great manager, the best I have ever had, and Celtic are lucky to have him and Henrik at the same time. The boss gave the club a new lease of life and brought the habit of winning back into the dressing-room.

"Maybe, before he arrived, if we were 2-0 up at the interval everyone would come in thinking the game was won and we would go out for the second half not properly prepared and end up drawing or losing.

"O'Neill doesn't allow that to happen. He is still as keen for things to be done properly as if the game was just about to start, and the players are now exactly the same.

"There is no slackness about the place on the day of a match until the three points have been won.

"Henrik has benefited from this and enjoys it under O'Neill. But it is not only him. Look at Bobby Petta – he is flying and has been since Martin arrived.

"There was a joke going around in his first season that we must have signed his twin instead of the real Bobby. But he is incredible, and I'm pleased for him because he is a really nice guy. Everyone could see from the moment he arrived that he was very skilful and tricky. He is now in the Holland squad and deserves his international recognition.

"The transformation in Bobby and other players is all down to man management from the boss. He receives great help from Steve Walford and John Robertson. They really are an incredible team, all with different strengths, and I think they will go on to do even better at Celtic.

"Henrik will also get better and I don't think it will be too far from the truth to say that Celtic will enjoy much more success in Scotland and some great results in Europe as long as Martin and Henrik are there.

"I hope they do achieve that because it will give me the perfect excuse to get over to Glasgow to watch them play, especially on the big European nights."

# eight my top six goals

HENRIK'S contribution to Celtic's treble was immense. At times, it seemed he was on a one-man crusade to pull the Hoops back from the abyss to the very top of Scotland's football pile.

As well as his goals in both cup finals, Larsson popped up time and time again with vital counters in tight matches to give Celts the winning edge they had lacked so badly in his year out with injury.

The super Swede's workrate during Celtic's glory season also astounded the media, the fans and his fellow players.

But it's goals that Larsson is most famous for. And in his dream season, there were 53 belters. Each one different, each one special and each one vital as Celtic ripped the crown of Scotland's top team from their bitter rivals Rangers.

Fans and pundits could wax lyrical all day about his greatest goals and which one was the most crucial – but what about the man himself? Here, Larsson picks his favourite six strikes from the season he went into the record books:

# Dundee United 1 Celtic 2, July 30, 2000

THIS was the match in which I scored my first goal of the season. I had waited a long time to get back in a Celtic shirt, and after playing for Sweden at the European Championships during the summer, I was feeling sharp and fit.

I think I had a good game overall and it was nice to cap it with a goal. A shot by Chris Sutton was blocked by a defender and the ball broke to me. I hit it with my left foot from about 20 yards and it went in.

It was a relief to give something back to Celtic after all the support they had given me during my injury.

# Celtic 6 Rangers 2, August 27, 2000

SCORING against Rangers is special. They are the ones the fans really remember you for. It was the first time we had played them this season and everyone was eager to see how we'd size up so for us to win so convincingly was utterly amazing.

"I scored our fourth and fifth but it was my first goal that was the most important. We had been 3-0 up in the first 13 minutes but Rangers had nearly pulled it back to 3-2. In that situation, the game can go either way, so it was important for us to get the initiative again.

"Five minutes into the second half Chris Sutton chested the ball down to me. I knocked the ball one side of Bert Konterman and ran past his other side. As Stefan Klos came out, I chipped the ball over him. I wasn't being flash – I thought it was the easiest way to score. It steadied us and what a great feeling."

# Celtic 3 Rangers 1, February 7, 2001

BEATING Rangers in the CIS Cup semi-final sticks in my mind. It was a really tough match. We had to play Rangers back-to-back, with the league game to follow on the Sunday, and they were fighting to get something from the season.

"Chris Sutton got our first and I scored our second after about 15 minutes. Johann Mjallby knocked the ball forward and I challenged for the ball with young defender Robert Malcolm.

"I managed to get it away from the defender. Then, as the 'keeper came out, I lobbed the ball over him, ran past and tapped it over the line. Later in the game I scored with a penalty kick to make sure we got into the final.

"Stefan Klos is a good goalie and I'm not making a habit of chipping him. Sometimes it's the only way."

# Dunfermline 0 Celtic 3, March 4, 2001

I DON'T suppose I've ever hit a better free-kick than the one in this game. It was very satisfying all round because it was one of those occasions when everybody seemed to have a good game at the same time.

"Some people have seen us as a battling side and it was nice to be able to show the sort of style we're capable of. The free-kick was awarded when Alan Thompson was brought down.

"The ball was about 25 yards out and I thought I'd try to hit it around the wall and into the top corner. It curled a lot and felt pretty good.

"They're the sort of shots when you just hit and hope but I knew as soon as I'd struck this that it was going in the right place."

# Celtic 1 Hearts 0, March 11, 2001

MY header in the quarter-final of the Scottish Cup wasn't very spectacular but it was important. It's awlays tough against Hearts and you have to fight for everything.

"We threw everything at them in the first half but they got players behind the ball and made it difficult. Then, just before half-time, Lubo Moravcik swung over a great cross which I managed to get on the end of.

"Antti Niemi is very good and he'd saved a couple from me earlier, so to get the breakthrough was a real relief. We didn't play brilliantly but we battled and that was important."

# Celtic 3 Kilmarnock 0, March 18, 2001

ALL of my goals in the CIS Cup final were special because it was a game we really wanted to win. My first was crucial but the third was my favourite.

"I got the ball just inside our half and chested it under control. There was a big gap behind the last defender and I knew if I could get past him I'd have a chance.

"That's what I did, and I ran towards goal. When I saw a Kilmarnock defender trying to get close to me on the right, I knew I didn't want to go that way.

I faked a shot to the left corner, and my former Celtic team-mate Gordon Marshall dived that way. Then I took the ball with the underside of my right boot, rolled it on to my other foot, and shot home."

# nine sweden

HENRIK LARSSON – or Henke, as he's best known back home – has been an international star for eight years now. During that time he's been a key figure in three World Cup campaigns as well as two European Championships so there is a whole generation of football fans in Sweden who can't remember when he wasn't a national figure.

It says a lot about the striker's ability and staying power that of the starting eleven when he made his debut – against Finland in a World Cup qualifier on October 13, 1993 – he is the only one still playing international football.

Then again, few of his countrymen have made such an impact on the Swedish public's consciousness as Henke.

He started as he meant to go on in Stockholm that night against the Finns, scoring the second goal in the home side's 3-2 win. It was a crucial strike.

The match was Sweden's penultimate qualifying tie and they ended up topping Group Six by a single point from Bulgaria, who finished a point clear of France by scoring the winner in Paris with the last kick of the final game in the section.

Larsson said: "The game was really important and I was nervous, which made the whole experience go quickly. My dream had been to play for my country but to score on my debut was just incredible and to top it all we qualified for the World Cup finals that day."

Although Sweden had performed creditably at Euro 92, when they had lost 3-2 to the Germans at the semi-final stage, they had hosted that tournament just as they had the World Cup in 1958, when they lost 5-2 to Brazil in the final.

The national team had not enjoyed any notable success outside their own country until the competition was held in the USA in 1994, when they were to come heartbreakingly close to going all the way.

For Henrik, too, it was to prove a tournament of mixed emotions as he experienced the best and worst of times. He had gone into it as a peripheral figure but emerged from it as one of the rising stars of the world game and, thanks to his dreadlocks, one of its more easily recognisable players.

Jonas Thern, a mainstay of the national side in those days and currently coach of Swedish Second Division side Varnamo, recalled: "It was difficult for Henrik at that time. He was very much in the early stages of his international career then and there were problems for him in the shape of Kennet Andersson and Martin Dahlin, who were ahead of him. There was also Tomas Brolin, who was such an attacking midfield player he might as well have been a forward.

"They were all established players in the side so it wasn't easy for youngsters to get their chance, no matter how talentd they were. Fortunately, Henrik always managed to do good things when he came on as a substitute and that made him a valuable member of our squad.

"In our opening group game against Cameroon, he showed a lot of confidence when he came on, even though we were 2-1 down at the time. He played a crucial role that day, firing in a shot from 30 yards which hit the bar. Dahlin scored from the rebound and that set us up for the rest of the tournament.

"That draw was vital because if we'd lost that day, it would have been all over for us."

Larsson then came on with eight minutes remaining of the 3-1 win over Russia but was thrilled, temporarily at least, to be included from the kick-off for the next game against bookies' favourites Brazil.

Unfortunately, for once the occasion seemed to get to the 22-year-old and he turned in what he considers to be the poorest performance of his career in front of 77,217 people at Detroit's Pontiac Stadium.

He said: "The worst game I have ever had personally was the one against Brazil. I'd done enough against Cameroon to get picked to start the match against Brazil, which was a great thrill for me. However, it was just one of those days when you know nothing is going your way.

"We managed to draw 1-1 but I didn't get into that game at all. It wasn't a bad game for Sweden but for Henrik Larsson it was a very bad day.

"It was no surprise when I was put on the bench for the whole of the next game against Saudi Arabia."

Sweden won that one 3-1 to set up a dramatic quarter-final clash with Romania and, more than any other, it was this game which accurately reflected the striker's big-match mettle.

The Eastern Europeans managed a late equaliser to take the match into extra-time, which is when Larsson was thrown on for the tiring Dahlin. Two hours didn't prove enough to separate the sides and so a place in the last four of the biggest sporting event in the world came to the ultimate test of nerve – the penalty shoot-out.

He said: "Patrik Andersson came over and told me I was going to be the sixth penalty taker, probably because they didn't think it would go that far. Unfortunately, our first penalty went over the bar, they missed one and that meant I had to take mine.

"I remember it like yesterday. I sat in the centre circle thinking about all the penalties I'd ever taken and trying to calm myself down. I hit it to the left, the keeper went right and the ball just sneaked in off the post. My heart stops even now when I see that film."

Perhaps as a result of his lacklustre performance in their group meeting, Henrik took no part in the semi-final against Brazil, which was settled by a late goal from Romario.

He was reinstated in the side for the third place play-off

against the Bulgarians in Los Angeles, and finally made his mark the way he does best.

The Swedes were already 2-0 up when, in the 37th minute, the phrase "and Larsson must score" entered the English language for the first time.

He said: "I found myself just inside their half. I think it could have been Kennet Anderssonn who played a square ball to me and I was able to touch it past the Bulgarian defender as they tried to push up on us.

"I had the goalkeeper to beat and, as I got into the penalty area, he came out and I pushed it to his right. He was down and beaten and the goal was in front of me.

"A Bulgarian defender came flying across and I dummied to shoot with my left. He tried to get in the way and, as he put his knee in the way, he simply fell over, which was pretty funny.

"I rounded him and all I had to do was roll the ball over the line which, luckily, I did. It was a good goal to score and it's one of my favourites. The feeling was incredible and getting that medal was unbelievable."

The final score that day was 4-0 and, although the Swedish national team has failed to consistently hit those heights since, Henrik remains their best hope of leading them to the World Cup finals in Japan and South Korea.

That's certainly the consensus among their current and former international stars.

Thern said: "Henrik had been criticised by some people in our media for not scoring as often for the national team as he does for Celtic but he answered them in the best possible way by scoring all the goals in our 4-0 win over Macedonia at the end of last season.

"That was special for him but it also kept us in with a chance of going back to the finals. That's important to the whole country after missing out the last time.

"In spite of his great finishing, I always love it when Henrik plays on the wing for Sweden. When he's used through the middle it's possible for defences to crowd him out but when he goes wide on either side he's usually only up against a full-back.

"There aren't too many defenders in the world who can stop him when he goes one-on-one because he has pace, he is skilful and he can do a lot of tricks with the ball."

Larsson was voted Sweden's Footballer of the Year in 1999 and his popularity in his native land continues to grow.

Former Rangers midfielder Thern, who opposed his friend during his memorable first campaign in Scotland, said: "Henrik is one of the most famous players here.

"Every Old Firm match is now shown live in Sweden and, because Henrik has been such a key player for them, most young kids in this country now wear Celtic tops with his name on the back, which is a huge tribute to him.

"When we were both in Glasgow, we each managed to win one or two games but those matches, plus our training exercises with Sweden, helped show to me just how hard he is physically.

"When you see him in a football strip, he doesn't look tough but there are few players stronger than him when it comes to holding you off with his arms."

Kennet Andersson was Larsson's strike partner for Sweden from 1993 until he retired from the international stage in April, 2001. The 34-year-old former Lazio, Bari and Bologna star, currently with Fenerbahce, has nothing but fond memories of their partnership.

He said: "Henrik was a dream to play alongside because he is so unselfish. He's typically Swedish in that way because he's always looking to do what is best for the tam.

"Even when he isn't scoring he's always dangerous because he's constantly trying to make runs and working hard. He puts in the same effort every time he goes on the park.

"He scores regularly, of course, but he's one of those guys who is effective even when he isn't, and that makes a difference if you're playing alongside him.

"I know he's been criticised for not managing more goals for the national team but that accusation has been levelled at every striker who has played for Sweden in recent years.

"However, Henrik gives 100 per cent each time he plays so the criticism means nothing. It won't bother him anyway.

"No-one expected him to be back playing at Euro 2000 so soon after breaking his leg so badly but that merely shows what an extraordinary person he is. No-one should ever question his mentality or his hunger to do well.

"Henrik is a star, but as well as being a complete player he's also a very nice boy. There isn't anything bad I can say about him. I've shared a room with him and he doesn't even snore!

"He's close to being the perfect striker but in spite of having too much skill. he never gets above himself or puts on any airs. He's a very down to earth person."

Sweden's assistant national coach Lars Lagerback believes the striker will be the name on everyone's lips as the 2002 World Cup in Japan and South Korea progresses.

Yes, Larsson-mania is set to move from the East End of Glasgow to the Far East.

That's how highly the Swedish staff rate him and they are pinning their hopes on Henrik being the man to lead his country to a successful World Cup campaign after their disappointing showing in Euro 2000.

The Swedes were knocked out at the first group stage following lacklustre performances against Belgium and Turkey, even though a superb Larsson goal inspired them to a battling display against eventual runners-up Italy. According to Lagerback – No.2 to national team boss Tommy Soderberg – part of the reason for the below-par showings was that, because of his leg break, Larsson had only played three games in the space of seven months before the tournament started and was nowhere near full match fitness.

But they know Henrik will be far better prepared for the big one and believe he will be ready to terrorise defences from around the world by showing the skills and ability we are lucky enough to see every week in the SPL.

Lagerback said: "I have a strong feeling Henrik is going to be a real star. He has the ability to do whatever he wants, no matter who he is playing against, and I would not be surprised if he upstages the world-famous names from France, Argentina, Brazil and elsewhere.

"He might not find the net in every game but contributes with assists all the time. People involved in football appreciate that just as much as the player who scores.

"We didn't perform particularly well at Euro 2000 and were criticised. There is nothing we can do about that now but I have no doubts we would have done much better with a fully fit Larsson. It was just unfortunate for us, and for Celtic, that he broke his leg in the season leading up to the championship. Although he came back he wasn't fully fit. We had to use him sparingly. We would have qualified for the next stage had Henrik been able to play in every game from the first whistle to the last whistle.

"Because he plays for Celtic should be of no concern to anyone. He has been criticised from certain areas for not moving to another country but that is negative talk and wrong.

"Henrik has nothing to prove and I think he made the right decision to stay in Glasgow. He spoke to us about it and we knew it was right for his career and his family to remain where he was, because he is happy and successful there. Henrik also knew that. He is an intelligent man."

When Lagerback talks about Larsson he doesn't use superlatives just for the sake of it – he's not that type of guy. He speaks honestly but goes on about Henrik because he knows the quality of the product and honours the adjectives he uses to describe it will not make him look foolish.

But Lars is not out on his own when it comes to his opinion on the country's top striker. The Swedish nation is warming to Larsson more and more and it has even been suggested he will end up beside the likes of tennis legend Bjorn Borg in the country's sporting Hall of Fame.

Soderberg and Lagerback are very concious of team spirit and teamwork, on and off the pitch. As well as having Larsson's talents on the pitch they believe his personality is vital to their success as he has an extremely positive attitude and influence on other squad members.

That is vital in international sides, especially when they are away from home for maybe a month during a World Cup, which can lead to boredom.

Eventually, boredom can spark a breaking of the rules and curfews as players are tempted for a night on the town for a few refreshments. Some even go to the lengths of climbing out their bedroom windows and down a drainpipe to escape and head for a good time.

Larsson isn't that sort and makes sure others aren't either. Sure, he might not be first up to grab the microphone and belt out

ABBA songs on the karaoke but he has other methods.

Lagerback revealed they rely heavily on him at such times. He said: "Henrik is a very nice person, one of the best I have ever worked with. And I mean that.

"He is marvellous to deal with. You never hear him complaining about a thing, and that is a marvellous quality. It is also good when younger guys see him behaving that way as the last thing we want in the national squad is unhappy players and bad influences.

"But we are not too strict with the players. We think it is better not to have any serious rules and leave them to behave responsibly, the way an adult should. If any problems arise – and I really can't remember any – we know we have men like Henrik ready to deal with them. He is respected and admired by every member of the squad.

"Tommy and myself try to arrange things when we are away on duty because we understand it is difficult to leave your family for so long – we feel it, too. So we try to keep everyone busy and make the trips as interesting as possible by taking advantage of the local sights and places of interest. It is good for morale and helps beat the boredom.

"Hopefully, if we get to the World Cup Finals, we will do well and enjoy the occasion to the full. The sights will be nice but the results will be the most important thing. As long as we're winning the camp will be happy, we will never forget that simple fact."

The vast majority of Scots, no matter which team they support, will reckon Sweden are extremely lucky to have a player like Larsson on their side. Can you see the scene if he had been able to pull on the dark blue of Scotland?

Just imagine how well off we would have been if the superstar had been born between the Solway Firth and the Shetland Isles. Or had a Scottish parent or grandparent. Picture him running behind the goal with his tongue hanging out, celebrating yet another great strike in front of the delirious Tartan Army as lion rampant flags and Saltires are waved in jubilation.

Our loss is Sweden's gain. But, amazingly, not everyone in that Scandinavian land truly appreciates the talent they have at their disposal. Indeed, some even seem to take a perverse delight in

138

criticising Henrik for his contribution to the national team.

You're probably thinking the great man can do no wrong, but in their eyes he can. Big time! The Swedish press and some fans have had a pop at Larsson over the past year or so for not doing as well as they thought he should have as the national team struggled to turn it on against so-called lesser nations.

Henrik was slaughtered with banner headlines as Sweden's inability to win games was blamed firmly on him.

And all of this happened last season... when the hot hitman was Europe's top striker as he banged in 53 goals for Celtic to help them to the Treble.

But Larsson's Swedish critics have defended their actions and feel they were right to single him out for harsh treatment.

Top journalist Christoffer Bjareborn didn't necessarily agree with the mood of the nation, but could understand their frustrations.

He explained: "The whole of our country appreciated Henrik working so hard after his leg break to get back to full fitness and play in Euro 2000. I remember a friendly against Spain just before the team left for their base that summer when around 30,000 people inside Gothenburg's stadium stood up to chant Henrik's name as he warmed up.

"It was great for everyone because nobody truly believed we would see him playing in Euro 2000. We all thought the injury was far too serious to come back quickly. We now know the medical staff at Celtic deserve much credit for his speedy recovery.

"But people have short memories and we were all disappointed by the showing in Euro 2000. The popular opinion was that the team played boring football and, as a result, Henrik plus some other players and the coaching staff came in for criticism.

"Then, after that, we couldn't really score against the likes of Macedonia and other small nations. Henrik got it again."

But he didn't have to suffer as much as Kennet Andersson. The big, gangly striker was given a really bad time by the press and fans because he just wasn't contributing anything, whereas Henrik was at least doing his best and doing some positive things to help others around him.

"The coach, Tommy Soderberg, hates hearing the players

being criticised and always comes out in public to defend them. He likes to have a happy atmosphere within the squad and will do everything he can to protect that and make sure his players do not become distracted by outside comments.

"But if you look at it sympathetically, Henrik and the others will always be compared to the Sweden squad of 1994 that finished third in the World Cup, which is regarded as one of the greatest achievements in more than 50 years.

"I know Henrik played in that tournament but he wasn't regarded as one of the top players. Guys such as Thomas Ravelli, Roland Nilsson and Patrik Andersson are the star footballers in the eyes of the Swedish people and it is hard to dislodge them from the front of their thoughts.

"Henrik, however, is regarded as one of the cornerstones of the current side along with Patrik Andersson, Freddie Ljundberg and Magnus Hedman. But I don't know if he will go down as one of the all-time greats. Perhaps it will happen if he does well in the 2002 World Cup Finals.

"But maybe Henrik will never be able to win the public over. He scored four goals against Moldova back in June in a World Cup qualifier, three of which came from the spot. He joked afterwards that everyone will say he can only score penalties.

"I think that was his way of making his point without being fierce in his criticism. He is too much of a man and a proud professional to start public arguments and always stresses the team is more important, not him or any other individual."

The main reason for the question marks against Larsson's name is the same one every player in this country has to put up with – namely, the accusation that he is is playing in Scotland, "that Mickey Mouse league".

Bjareborn at least makes the effort to come to Scotland to watch Larsson and Johan Mjallby play as often as possible… and understands the game here is nowhere near as easy as people in his homeland make out. But he fears his valuation will never be shared by the majority in Sweden.

Christoffer said: "If Henrik had scored that amount of goals for Manchester United, Arsenal or Liverpool he would be treated as a truly great sporting hero. But people think Scotland is second rate. It was the same for Henrik when he played in Holland for

Feyenoord, with people saying it must be easy to score so many goals.

"I know Henrik and Johan are forever telling people the SPL is highly competitive, but the public simply won't believe them. Part of the reason is most of the European football we see here is from England, Italy and Spain. Scotland doesn't feature regularly and we have to rely on the newspapers for information about Celtic.

"I make the effort to go and see Celtic and I know it is tough in Scotland. There are players earning a living there who play regularly for Holland, Denmark, Australia, Norway and other top countries, so they can't all be wrong.

"However, I think some of the minds here are made up and won't be changed. Believe me, I do try to get other people from my country over to see Scottish football but they are difficult to persuade. It's a pity, because I know they would enjoy the football and the hospitality of Scotland. Also, Henrik and Johan always make me feel very welcome whenever I visit. I think they appreciate that I make the effort.

"When I talk to Henrik, even after the four years he has been in Glasgow, he sometimes still finds it hard to believe the amount of attention he receives on a daily basis. It really is incredible. When we found out in Sweden that cutting his dreadlocks off for a new short hairstyle made the front pages of the newspapers in Scotland and that they ran competitions to win one of the dreadlocks, we couldn't believe it.

"If that happened in Sweden the country would come to a standstill in a state of shock at all the fuss. Nobody would get that kind of attention for such a routine thing. But it emphasises the point of how important Henrik is to Scotland and what an ambassador he is."

Larsson will retire from top-level football when his contract with Celtic expires in the summer of 2004. He will return with his family to Helsingborg and has yet to decide what he will do with the rest of his life.

Bjareborn feels there will be a public campaign to keep him involved in football in some capacity and hopes Henrik will be swayed by the lobbying.

He said: "We all know he plans to come back here in a couple of years' time but hope he doesn't walk away from the game for good. Although he has been criticised he is still very respected and the people of Sweden know we will be better off with him than without him.

"I suppose coaching young kids would be perfect for Henrik and it would please a lot of the young footballers who are ready to become stars of the future. There can't be too many better around than Henrik to do that kind of thing. And if our country doesn't make a move to get him, then I'm sure Scotland will."

Certainly, if international players were available for transfer, Craig Brown would probably raid every bank in Scotland for the cash to secure Larsson's services.

Unlike fans in this country, the Scotland coach was well aware of the Swedish goal machine before he decided to become a Celtic player.

As the head of our national team it's Brown's duty to be informed about the capabilities of potential opponents. He had put the striker under the microscope long before the likes of Walter Smith and Jim Jefferies had to.

Quite apart from his natural inclination to absorb footballing data, the fact that Sweden were drawn in Scotland's World Cup qualifying group ensured Craig had a working knowledge of Henrik while he was still a Feyenoord player.

As mentioned elsewhere, Larsson's problems with the Dutch club contributed to his most fallow period for the international side and he started just one of his country's 10 ties in Group 4, the 1-0 win over Estonia in Stockholm.

Other than that, Henrik made just three appearances as a substitute, including an electrifying 22 minutes in the 1-0 defeat by Scotland at Ibrox when he ran his teammate-to-be Jackie McNamara ragged as the Swedes staged a storming fightback.

Henrik scored his only goal of that campaign in a 5-1 rout of Belarus. Though they were technically the best team in the group, Sweden contrived to miss out on France 98, finishing third behind Austria and Scotland.

Even so, Brown was a Larsson fan long before it became fashionable. He said: "I've watched Henrik often over the years and the role he fulfils for his country is very similar to the one at club level. The first time I saw him was in a video of a Dutch

Cup tie when he scored an excellent goal for Feyenoord.

"More recently, I thought he had a superb Euro 2000 despite not being fully fit. He scored a terrific goal against the Italians, which is always difficult."

It's hardly a state secret that Scotland's main problem since Denis Law was in his pomp has been the lack of a reliable, prolific scorer. Our goals come in trickles rather than floods.

In the last five years or so that trickle has become a drought. Brown freely admits he wishes Larsson had been born in Hamilton rather than Hagaborg.

He sighed: "In recent times Ally McCoist has been our top scorer with 19 goals from 61 appearances. But, of course, he's no longer available.

"What a difference having a player like Henrik would make. As things stand, we go out for matches hoping to score. With Larsson in the side you'd be expecting to get goals and that makes a major difference to your mindset.

"I was down at Loftus Road in July 2001 to watch him make his first appearance of the season against Queen's Park Rangers. Of course, he scored in the very first minute.

"I turned to the Sheffield Wednesday manager Peter Shreeve who was sitting next to me, and said: 'My God, he's just starting where he left off'.

"That in itself is remarkable because, like many people in the game, I thought Henrik might never play again after that terrible leg-break in Lyon.

"The fact that he's not only playing, but playing at the very peak of his powers week in week out, says a lot about him as a player and as a man.

"Some people suspected he couldn't score for the Swedish national team the way he does for Celtic but that's nonsense, as his record proves."

And Larsson continues to defy the few critics he has left, scoring the opener and making the two others in Sweden's 3-0 win over South Africa on August 15. Some things never change.

# ten champions league

HOW do you follow a tremendous treble? By boldly going where no Celtic team had gone before and finally, after 10 years trying, entering the Champions League.

How can you possibly top a record-breaking 53-goal season? Well, scoring in the very first minute of your first match is a good way to start.

For Henrik Larsson and for Celtic Football Club, 2001/02 was always going to be the real proving ground. For a club which hadn't won consecutive titles for 20 years the championship remained the priority.

As for the Scottish Cup, it hadn't been successfully defended since 1989, when Joe Miller's goal saw off Rangers.

It was essential that Martin O'Neill and his players emphasised their position as kings of the hill and let everyone know that the previous campaign was not merely a blip in Rangers' long-term dominance of Scottish football.

Celtic also hadn't been involved in Europe after Christmas since 1980. So, far from being sated by their treble success there was no shortage of targets for these players to aim for.

Just 13 months earlier, before the appointment of O'Neill as manager and before Henrik had proved beyond doubt that he was an even better player than he had been before his horrific double fracture, no Celtic supporter would have dared to dream they would be in this position.

Yet on August 23, 2001, in a hall in Monaco packed with football celebrities and executives from all over Europe, the name of Celtic joined those of the continent's most famous clubs as they were drawn out of their little red plastic balls. Then the letter D was picked from a green plastic ball. As one of the eight bottom seeds, Celtic found themselves in the same group as Juventus, Porto and Rosenborg.

After a summer or relative inactivity, four new signings were made to bolster the squad. Alan Stubbs, Ramon Vega, Stephane Mahe, Mark Burchill and the unpopular Eyal Berkovic left, replaced by Bobo Balde from Toulouse, Coventry City's John Hartson, Momo Sylla from St Johnstone and Steve Guppy, another capture from O'Neill's old club, Leicester City.

As for Henrik, he and Joos Valgaeren were allowed an extra week's rest following their exertions for Sweden and Belgium respectively in June so his first match back in the hoops was at Loftus Road against Queen's Park Rangers.

The combination of exiled fans and the usual travelling support meant the stadium was full to witness Larsson carry on in the same manner as he had finished the previous year.

Barely 40 seconds had elapsed after the kick-off when Alan Thompson spotted the striker's typically intelligent run into the penalty area. His chip forward was as well judged as Larsson's finish, as he dinked the ball over the advancing 'keeper and into the unguarded net.

Like so many of his goals, it was beautifully simple and simply beautiful. As usual, the famous tongue came out in celebration and, possibly, relief.

For strikers, even the best of them (and Henrik has surely earned his place among the elite division), the first goal of a new season always feels special. Like a golfer holing his first putt in a tournament, it soothes the nerves and reminds them not only that this is what they do best, but also that they can still do it.

After that, there was no looking back and he scored the only goal of the game from the penalty spot as Sunderland were sent

146

packing at Parkhead.

When the phoney war ended Celtic unravelled their 37th league championship flag and St Johnstone were put to the sword at Parkhead.

Perhaps the only surprise that evening was that Henrik didn't score in the 3-0 win, countryman Johan Mjallby and Paul Lambert with his first senior double doing the needful.

Even more surprising was the fact he didn't find the net at Old Trafford when Celtic beat Sir Alex Ferguson's Manchester United 4-3 in a testimonial match for Welsh winger Ryan Giggs.

In front of a highly-charged crowd of 66,957 – 15,000 tickets had been snapped up by the visitors – Celtic were two goals up inside four minutes through Chris Sutton and Neil Lennon.

Their pride stung, United, playing their strongest side which included record signings Juan Sebastian Veron and Ruud van Nistelrooy, fought back. It was game on, and any pretence of this being a mere friendly was forgotten.

Tackles were of the crunching variety and there were several eyeball-to-eyeball confrontations. David Beckham even received a playful slap from Sutton for his trouble.

It was a thrilling match, as good a friendly as anyone present had ever seen. Van Nistelrooy pulled one back for the home side before Lambert restored the two-goal cushion by drilling in a superb 20-yarder.

That goal came after Larsson had eluded Jaap Stam during the build-up on the left. The Dutchman is one of the world's top defenders but he had no answer to the speed of thought and movement shown by his opponent that night.

Veron pulled one back with the goal of the evening before Lubomoir Moravcik made it four with a trademark free-kick. And although van Nistelrooy netted again and then hit the bar, Celtic were worthy winners.

The victory was of incalculable worth to O'Neill's side. Taking on the club which had dominated the Premiership for seven of the previous nine years and beating them in their own backyard sent the squad's confidence through the roof.

The following Saturday, a typically tough fixture at Kilmarnock was decided by a solitary goal by Larsson, running on to a beautifully judged Sutton chip to drive it beyond

Gordon Marshall 14 minutes from time

An interested spectator was Co Adriaanse, coach of Celtic's opponents in the final qualifying round for the Champions' League, Ajax Amsterdam.

He said: "I am not impressed by John Hartson. I have no fears that my defenders can handle his threat. But Larsson is a danger. He is quick, intelligent and stays cool in front of goal.

"He only got one chance and took it. You need two players for him because if you put him one against one, he is too dangerous."

The Swede himself was under no illusions as to the importance of going through. He said: "There is no doubt Celtic should be in the Champions' League every year because we are a big club with a massive support. With a club this size, you always want to show it off in the biggest tournament.

"When I arrived I, didn't know what to expect. I didn't know that much about Celtic's background or the potential but you soon realise a club of this size must be successful.

"We played well against Bordeaux last year and were unlucky not to go through but in Europe there are a lot of narrow margins and it's important we do the little things right, like defending as a team. The rest will follow."

In spite of their impressive form under O'Neill, Celtic's depressing European record saw them go into the match in the Amsterdam ArenA as 11-4 outsiders. Bookmakers William Hills even offered 5-6 against them managing to score at any point in the game. The odds layers were to regret their generosity.

Bobby Petta fired Celtic ahead after just seven minutes after Ajax goalkeeper Fred Grim had flapped at a Sutton cross. Didier Agathe made it two when he sprinted on to a perfect first-time pass from Larsson.

Although Shota Arveladze cut the deficit in half, Sutton bulleted home a header from Agathe's cross to make it 3-1. Henrik could have had a hat-trick but his all-round play was superb as Celtic turned in their most accomplished performance on European soil for almost 30 years.

His countryman Zlatan Ibrahimovic, a £5million signing from Malmo that summer, was in awe of Henrik afterwards, even though they had something of an altercation in the dying minutes.

The 19-year-old said: "We did have a bit of an argument near the end but it was nothing serious. I didn't even hear what Henrik said to me.

"Overall, though, I have a feeling we were scared and could only play sideways as a result. Henrik was really, really good and did so much to help Celtic win."

Larsson claimed: "Ajax have a lot of talented young players but they lack the routine we have with the established international in every position.

"Anything can happen in the return but it sure looks good for us going into that second leg. I was also really satisfied with my own performance."

Three days later, Hearts turned up at Parkhead and defended for 90 minutes in a damage-limitation exercise. The Tynecastle outfit had haemorrhaged 20 goals in six meetings with Celtic the previous season and manager Craig Levein unapologetically set out with the sole intention of avoiding a hammering.

However, even with 10 men behind the ball, Henrik's genius was able to find a way through. He opened the scoring with a free-kick on the stroke of half-time and closed with with an exquisite goal, turning on a sixpence to control a Hartson flick before swivelling away from marker Kevin McKenna to rifle an unsaveable shot behind Antti Niemi.

A nervous, goalless draw at newly-promoted Livingston was excused by players having half a mind on the Ajax return.

Henrik even failed to convert a late penalty, his netbound shot deflected over by the flailing leg of Javier Broto. But Rangers failed to capitalise on that slip-up, drawing 2-2 with Hibs at Ibrox that evening, so his miss wasn't as significant as it might have been.

Not that it dented Henrik's confidence in his own spot-kick technqique. He pointed out he had missed two penalties in the league the previous season – against Hearts and Dunfermline, but had carried on to slot home countless vital penatlties. Imagine, he could have scored 55 goals that season!

On the eve of the crucial second leg against Ajax, Martin O'Neill claimed that holding a 3-1 lead wouldn't make it awk-ward for his players in terms of their approach to the game. But that didn't prove to be the case.

Celtic defended too deep in the first half, allowing the

opposition time and space on the ball. Uncharacteristcally, the team seemed somewhat unsure of themselves.

Their normal pressing game was largely abandoned and they spent most of the first half chasing shadows. Rab Douglas made several fine saves but Ajax should have had more to show for their supremacy than a solitary goal from the Brazilian, Wamberto.

Fortunately, the manager steadied his team at the interval and they looked more solid for the remaining 45 minutes without ever producing the type of ammunition Larsson was craving until the last few minutes.

The final whistle was greeted with roars of relief. The evening could be put down to experience – part of the steep learning curve the Champions' League represents.

The following morning, O'Neill and his star striker set off for Monaco. The manager was there to witness the draw for the first group phase, while Henrik was to collect the prestigious Golden Shoe, awarded to him for being Europe's top scorer the previous season. With potentially hazardous trips to Italy, Norway and Portugal looming on the horizon, every Celtic fan will be hoping the Shoe fits.

Both club and player have already waited too long to make their mark at that rarefied level. The draw, while no pushover, was not as treacherous as it could have been, allowing Celtic fans to walk on with hope in their hearts.

With just two more full seasons left before he leaves to return to his native Sweden – and no one should doubt his word that he will go when that time comes – the belief is there that, at the very least, solid foundations for a serious challenge on the continent can be laid this season.

When the draw was made in Monte Carlo, William Hills immediately offered 3-1 for either Manchester United, Arsenal or Liverpool to lift the trophy. Celtic, by contrast, were quoted at 40-1.

With Larsson in full flow, backed by the most potent Celtic side for two decades, there will have been a few takers.

After all, in his life and his career, Henrik has made a habit of prevailing against all odds.

# HENRIK LARSSON
## CAREER DETAILS

Date of birth: 20/09/71
Place of birth: Helsingborg, Sweden
Position: Forward
Nationality: Sweden
International caps: 50
International goals: 11

Signed 25/07/1997  for £650,000 from Feyenoord
Celtic squad number: 7

## THE SEASON SO FAR... 2001/2002

| DATE | COMP | SCORE | LARSSON GOALS |
|------|------|-------|---------------|
| 28/07 | SPL | Celtic 3 St Johnstone 0 | 0 |
| 04/08 | SPL | Kilmarnock 0 Celtic 1 | 1 |
| 08/08 | EC | Ajax 1 Celtic 3 | 0 |
| 11/08 | SPL | Celtic 2 Hearts 0 | 2 |
| 15/08 | Internat | Sweden 3 South Africa 0 | 1 |
| 18/08 | SPL | Livingston 0 Celtic 0 | 0 |
| 22/08 | EC | Celtic 0 Ajax 1 | 0 |
| 25/08 | SPL | Hibernian 1 Celtic 4 | 1 |

# HENRIK LARSSON
# CELTIC CAREER STATS

## SEASON 1997/98

| League | | Scottish Cup | | League Cup | | Europe | |
|---|---|---|---|---|---|---|---|
| A | G | A | G | A | G | A | G |
| 34 (1) | 16 | 4 (0) | 0 | 5 (0) | 3 | 2 (0) | 0 |

**TOTAL APPEARANCES: 45 (1)**          **TOTAL GOALS: 19**

## SEASON 1998/99

| League | | Scottish Cup | | League Cup | | Europe | |
|---|---|---|---|---|---|---|---|
| A | G | A | G | A | G | A | G |
| 35 (0) | 28 | 5 (0) | 5 | 0 (0) | 0 | 7 (0) | 4 |

**TOTAL APPEARANCES: 47**          **TOTAL GOALS: 37**

## SEASON 1999/2000

| League | | Scottish Cup | | League Cup | | Europe | |
|---|---|---|---|---|---|---|---|
| A | G | A | G | A | G | A | G |
| 8 (1) | 7 | 0 (0) | 0 | 0 (0) | 0 | 4 (0) | 5 |

**TOTAL APPEARANCES: 12 (1)**          **TOTAL GOALS: 12**

## SEASON 2000/01

| League | | Scottish Cup | | League Cup | | Europe | |
|---|---|---|---|---|---|---|---|
| A | G | A | G | A | G | A | G |
| 37 (0) | 35 | 6 (0) | 9 | 2 (0) | 5 | 5 (0) | 4 |

**TOTAL APPEARANCES: 50**          **TOTAL GOALS: 53**

## TOTAL*

| League | | Scottish Cup | | League Cup | | Europe | |
|---|---|---|---|---|---|---|---|
| A | G | A | G | A | G | A | G |
| 114 (2) | 86 | 15 (0) | 14 | 7 (0) | 8 | 18 (0) | 13 |

**TOTAL APPEARANCES: 154 (2)**          **TOTAL GOALS: 121**

* up to and including season 2000/01